Best Walks in the Welsh Bord

C000082493

Best Walks in the Welsh Borders

Simon Whaley

Frances Lincoln

Frances Lincoln Ltd
4 Torriano Mews
Torriano Avenue
London NW5 2RZ
www.franceslincoln.com

First published in Great Britain by Frances Lincoln 2007
Copyright © Simon Whaley 2007
Designed by Kevin Brown at park44.com

British Library Cataloguing in Publication data
A catalogue record for this book is available from the British Library.

Printed and bound in Singapore

ISBN 978 0 7112 2766 8

9 8 7 6 5 4 3 2 1

frontispiece: Looking towards Sugar Loaf, Walk 34

Contents

South Borders   189

Acknowledgements

This collection of walks would be poorer if it were not for the help, advice and companionship I have encountered along the way. The information about The Wrekin in Shropshire, for example, came from a good friend and fellow writer, George Evans. He is someone who, some 20 years into his retirement, still manages to climb this local peak regularly, and I can only hope that I am as active on the hills as he is when I achieve his tender age.

Walking is an activity that can be done on your own or with others, depending on your mood, and I'd like to thank the people who accompanied me on my way and also managed to put up with my 'hang on a minute, I just need to write this bit down' comments, without getting too frustrated. They include Wendy Coombey and her daughters, Jessica and Lydia, and my mother who thought she was going for a 4.8km (3 mile) walk, not an 8km (5 mile) one. I'd also like to thank Annie, Roger, Holly and Ruth Brookes, who allowed me to accompany them on one of their favourite walks, number 26, Croft Castle.

Special thanks also need to go to the rights of way officers at the various local authorities in this region who answered my queries so efficiently. These include Eifon Jones in the Brecon Beacons, Marcus Punter in Powys, Vincent Playdon in Herefordshire and John Marchant in Wrexham. I would also like to thank Betty Maura-Cooper of Hay town council, and all the staff at the various tourist information centres, who provided a wealth of background information, confirming bus routes, timetables and opening times for me.

Finally, I'd like to thank you, the purchaser of this book. I hope you find not only these walks but also the Welsh borders as a whole as beautiful as I do and that you are inspired to explore the area even further. I might even bump into you somewhere along the way. If you have any comments, about either a specific route or the book in general, please contact me at welshborderwalks@simonwhaley.co.uk.

Simon Whaley
September 2006

Introduction

The Welsh borders provide breathtaking and peaceful walking opportunities. While the hills may not be as high as those in Snowdonia or the Brecon Beacons, the views from the peaks are just as worthy. Yes, the area has its beauty spots, but it is generally quiet, and relative solitude can be found, even on a bank holiday weekend.

The Welsh borders have had a turbulent history, but, fortunately, things are much quieter now. It has always been a popular area for walking, particularly with long-distance walkers who have trudged along Offa's Dyke on its 285km (177 mile) route from Prestatyn on the North Wales coast to Chepstow on the Bristol Channel. Today there are more long-distance routes, including the Wye Valley walk and the Severn Way, which follow the meanderings of these two important rivers through the region.

Only when you begin to explore the area will you really appreciate the wealth of walking opportunities that exist here, and this book is designed to whet your appetite. I have tried to include a few suggestions for additional walks at the end of each individual walk to inspire you further should you wish to explore the area in greater detail.

People may rush through the Welsh borders for the more exciting scenery of Snowdonia in the north and the Brecon Beacons in the south, but the borders are certainly not boring. Pistyll Rhaeadr (see Walk 6) is one of Wales's most scenic and highest waterfalls, with a drop larger than that of the Niagara Falls, yet it lies less than 32.2km (20 miles) from the English border town of Oswestry.

The Elan Valley houses several reservoirs, providing fresh water to Birmingham. However, no pumps are used to transport it this distance: gravity does all the hard work. Barnes Wallis carried out research in the area to learn how to use explosives in order to destroy a dam, the remains of which are still visible today (see Walk 23). Only when he understood this, could he go on to develop the bouncing bomb.

The tranquil Clun Valley (see Walk 19) inspired A.E. Housman to write some of his most popular poetry, while the composer Edward Elgar enjoyed fishing at Mordiford in Herefordshire (see Walk 33). And on the edge of the Black Mountains stands Sugar Loaf (Walk 34), an iconic hill in the Abergavenny skyline and one that Rudolph Hess was allowed to climb frequently for exercise when he was held as a prisoner of war nearby during the Second World War.

Because the borders are relatively quiet, with no major motorways or dual carriageways, much of the area provides excellent habitats for wildlife. Birds of prey are beginning to thrive again, and buzzards are plentiful, with peregrine falcons nesting in a few of the rockier outcrops. The red kite has been successfully reintroduced into the mid-Wales area, and numbers of this handsome bird can be seen around the Elan Valley area. Meanwhile, in Herefordshire the water vole has recently been re-introduced to the River Dore.

GETTING THERE

Most of the walks start from some sort of car parking area, as this is how most people travel these days. However, in recognition of those who prefer to use public transport or those who are using it as a break from driving, public transport options are noted where appropriate. Although this region is not over-burdened with railway lines, the Manchester–Cardiff line provides access to the area from Shrewsbury southwards. The single-track Heart of

Wales Railway Line is served by an average of only four trains a day, but it is useful for some of the more rural spots in the mid- and south border areas. Further information about public transport is identified in each route description (contact telephone numbers may be for dedicated travel lines in the area or the switchboard for the operating company running the service number quoted), but general information can be found using Traveline West Midlands at (www.travelinemidlands.co.uk) or Traveline Cymru (www.traveline-cymru.org.uk). Alternatively, you can ring the Traveline service on 0870 608 2608, when you may need to ask to be put through to the right regional area, depending on where you are calling from.

MAPS

You should carry a map with you at all times when you are out walking and know how to use it. The maps provided in this book should not be used on their own. They are merely sketch maps and are not drawn to scale, although they will help you identify the route more easily when you are looking at the corresponding Ordnance Survey map. The orange-covered Explorer maps are better than the pink-covered Landranger maps because they are more detailed. At a scale of 1:25,000, they are the equivalent to 4cm (2½in) on the map representing 1km (1 mile) on the ground.

Each route identifies exactly which map in this series is needed for that particular route, but you should bear in mind that things on the ground can change. I have tried to provide quite detailed route descriptions, pointing out whether it should be a wooden or metal gate in front of you, whether the stile is on the right- or left-hand side of a gate, and which side of a road to follow to use a pedestrian path where appropriate, to give you confidence when following a route. However, farmers often replace fences and gates, and wooden structures become metal ones or fields may be enlarged as hedges or fences are removed. Forestry organisations

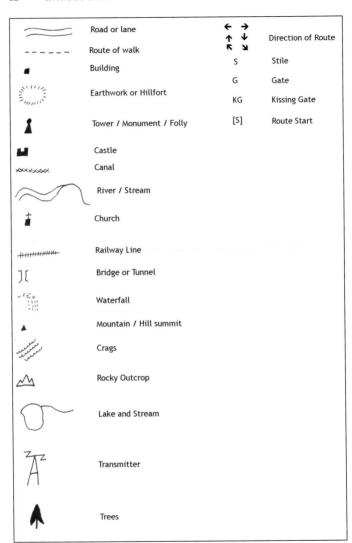

～～～	Road or lane	← → ↑ ↓ ↖ ↘	Direction of Route
– – – – –	Route of walk	S	Stile
◾	Building	G	Gate
💥	Earthwork or Hillfort	KG	Kissing Gate
🗼	Tower / Monument / Folly	[S]	Route Start
🏰	Castle		
xxxxxxxx	Canal		
～～～	River / Stream		
✝	Church		
+++++++++	Railway Line		
] [	Bridge or Tunnel		
💧	Waterfall		
▲	Mountain / Hill summit		
〰〰	Crags		
⋀⋀	Rocky Outcrop		
◯	Lake and Stream		
📡	Transmitter		
🌲	Trees		

Key to map symbols

have been known to plant where there were once clearings and to clear trees where a thick forest once existed. There will also be occasions when footpaths are legally diverted because of the presence of livestock or because a path has become unsafe. At all times, follow the instructions given on the diversion.

OPEN ACCESS

Since 2005 more than 1,618,800 hectares (4 million acres) of the English and Welsh countryside have been opened up for the public to enjoy. The land is known as Open Access land, and the legislation allows anyone to access areas of mountain, moor and uncultivated countryside in a controlled manner, where before they were denied. It should not be thought of as a 'right to roam', as it has been popularised by the media, but more of a managed access on foot to open land.

Individuals still have responsibilities when accessing such land, and the Countryside Agency produced an excellent leaflet, *Countryside Access and the New Right*, which can be downloaded from their website (www.countrysideaccess.gov.uk). This details the responsibilities that we all have, as well as outlining extra guidelines for dog owners.

New Ordnance Survey maps shade Open Access land in yellow to help walkers identify where such land exists, and many of the routes in this book cross Open Access land. A logo (a brown man walking on a brown hill with a white background) can often be seen at many points where paths enter Open Access land, and you may also see a similar logo with a red line through it, when leaving such land. This logo also appears on the new Ordnance Survey maps.

Open Access land is not necessarily open all the time. Legally, owners are able to close such land for up to 28 days throughout the year, and they are entitled to apply for longer periods of closure if

Distance marker on Montgomery Canal

they have a valid reason, such as wildlife management or issues of public safety. Both Natural England (www.countrysideaccess.gov.uk) and the Countryside Council for Wales (www.ccw.gov.uk) have excellent websites, which should be checked before you undertake any of the routes in this book to make sure that no restrictions are in place when you want to visit. Both sites allow you to click on a map and zoom into the area where you wish to walk, and any restrictions currently in place or likely to be imposed in the immediate future will be highlighted.

PERMISSIVE PATHS

Some routes in this book use permissive paths. These are not legal rights of way but routes that are created by kind and generous landowners, who are happy to allow responsible walkers to cross their land. They may not appear on your Ordnance Survey map. Importantly though, because they are not legal rights of way, the landowner can close them at any time, preventing access. Their reasons may be similar to those mentioned above in connection with Open Access, such as wildlife management issues or for safety. The important point is to follow any instructions or notices you may see regarding the permissive footpath at all times.

SAFETY

Continuing with the theme of taking heed of your surroundings, it is important to remember that walking in remote rural areas can be dangerous. Paths may run alongside craggy outcrops with hidden large drops, so keep children and dogs under control at all times. Particularly after heavy rainfall, rivers and streams can swell, swamping riverside paths. Rocks and boulders can become slippery, and even when you are wearing proper walking boots it may be difficult to maintain a good foothold. Always wear sensible clothing when you are out walking and carry extra layers and waterproofs, even if you don't think that you will need them when you set out.

Extreme care should be taken in the immediate vicinity of waterfalls. It is possible to get very close to the falls, but only with extreme caution and if local conditions make it possible. Never play about at the extreme foot of the waterfall, because debris flowing over the top could hit you as it falls.

Always take care when crossing rural roads. While there may not be any motorways in the region, unless the road is actually passing through a built-up area, the maximum speed limit on many of these roads is 60mph (which is the equivalent of nearly 100kph). Never assume that because a road is single track and quiet it is safe to let dogs off leads or children run free.

WHEN TO WALK

Each of the routes described in the book can be tackled comfortably in one day. However, a sensible approach is needed at all times. During the summer months paths will be drier and easier to walk along and rivers will be easier to explore. Yet on a clear, crisp, sunny winter's day the view from a relatively small hill can be truly spectacular. However, in these conditions, you should allow extra time to complete the walk because paths may be wet and slippery.

Recent weather patterns seem to suggest that Britain will be subject to more frequent sudden changes in the weather and more extreme weather. Heavy rainfall can completely change the character of a stream for several hours. It takes just two days for the heavy rain falling on the Cambrian Mountains in mid-Wales to find its way to the River Severn and its tributaries and then to travel the 113km (70 miles) to Shrewsbury.

USING THIS GUIDE BOOK

I have tried to provide as much information and detail as possible for each route, particularly relating to refreshments, toilets, public transport, nearby places of interest and local tourist attractions. However, any of these can be subject to change, and it is always sensible to double-check opening times and transport options yourself before you set out to tackle a walk. Having said that, I hope that this guidebook will help you explore the wonder of the Welsh borders and tempt you to come back, time and time again.

GRADING THE WALKS

I have graded each of the walks to fall into one of three categories: easy, moderate or invigorating. In reality, there are few peaks in the Welsh borders that are higher than 610m (2,000ft), and therefore any walk that I have labelled as 'invigorating'

Seat overlooking the Vale of Clwyd

should be well within the means of any average fit and healthy person. The basic grading system is:

- Easy: between 4.8 and 8km (3–5 miles) and relatively flat
- Moderate: between 8 and 11.3km (5–7 miles) or involving some hill climbing.
- Invigorating: between 11.3 and 19.3km (7–12 miles) or involving several steep sections

The distances quoted have been calculated by tracing the route on the map. They don't, therefore, take into account the extra distance that will be covered when walking up- and downhill. Grading walks is also a subjective matter. One person's 'easy' might be another's 'invigorating'. The important point, though, is to enjoy them. It's not a race, which is why I haven't given suggested timescales for tackling them. The Welsh borders should be savoured, not rushed. Relax and admire the views.

Walk number and name	Distance	Grading
North Borders		
Walk 1: Moel Famau	11km (6¾ miles)	Invigorating
Walk 2: Llangollen	13km (8 miles)	Invigorating
Walk 3: Bangor-is-y-coed	5km (3 miles)	Easy
Walk 4: Ceiriog Valley	12km (7½ miles)	Moderate
Walk 5: Ellesmere	10km (6¼ miles)	Moderate
Walk 6: Pistyll Rhaeadr	9km (5½ miles)	Moderate
Walk 7: Grinshill	5km (3 miles)	Easy
Walk 8: Lake Vyrnwy	18.5km (11½ miles)	Invigorating
Walk 9: Breidden Hills	5km (3 miles)	Moderate
Mid-Borders		
Walk 10: The Wrekin	6km (3¾ miles)	Moderate
Walk 11: Welshpool	6.5km (4 miles)	Easy
Walk 12: Stiperstones	5km (3 miles)	Easy
Walk 13: Montgomery	9km (5½ miles)	Moderate
Walk 14: The Long Mynd	10.5km (6½ miles)	Moderate
Walk 15: Wenlock Edge	6km (3¾ miles)	Easy
Walk 16: Brown Clee Hill	10km (6¼ miles)	Moderate
Walk 17: Bishop's Castle	11.5km (7¼ miles)	Invigorating
Walk 18: Kerry Ridgeway	11km (6¾ miles)	Moderate
Walk 19: Clun	14km (8¾ miles)	Invigorating
Walk 20: Craven Arms	15.5km (9½ miles)	Invigorating
Walk 21: Knucklas	8km (5 miles)	Easy
Walk 22: Mortimer Forest	16.5km (10¼ miles)	Invigorating

Walk number and name	Distance	Grading
South Borders		
Walk 23: Elan Valley	11.5km (7¼ miles)	Invigorating
Walk 24: Llandrindod Wells	9.5km (6 miles)	Moderate
Walk 25: Water-Break-its-Neck	5km (3 miles)	Easy
Walk 26: Croft Castle	8.5km (5¼ miles)	Easy
Walk 27: Hergest Ridge	12km (7½ miles)	Invigorating
Walk 28: Aberedw	12km (7½ miles)	Invigorating
Walk 29: Dinmore Hill	4.5km (2¾ miles)	Easy
Walk 30: Dorstone	8.75km (5½ miles)	Moderate
Walk 31: Hay Bluff	15.5km (9½ miles)	Invigorating
Walk 32: Abbey Dore	7.75km (4¾ miles)	Easy
Walk 33: Mordiford	12.5km (7¾ miles)	Moderate
Walk 34: Sugar Loaf	12km (7½ miles)	Invigorating
Walk 35: Symonds Yat	10.5km (6½ miles)	Moderate

Overleaf: River Dee

North Borders

WALK 1 | Moel Famau

At the summit of Moel Famau are the remains of the Jubilee Tower. Built in 1810 to mark George III's golden jubilee, it was never completed. It was hoped that a pyramid 46m (150ft) tall would top the summit, but ferocious storms in the 1860s caused severe damage. A few minor repairs in the 1970s made it safe, and it now provides a wonderful viewing platform some 9m (30ft) high. Climb to the summit on a clear day and expect to see Liverpool, the Rivers Mersey and Dee, the North Wales coast, Snowdonia and the Vale of Clywd.

The summit forms part of an 810 hectare (2,000 acre) country park administered by Denbighshire Countryside Service. This invigorating walk explores some of this as well as a section of the Offa's Dyke national trail.

Walk category: invigorating | Length: about 11km (6¾ miles) | Map: Explorer Sheet 265, Clwydian Range, Prestatyn, Mold and Ruthin | Parking and starting point: Moel Famau Country Park car park, small charge; grid ref: SJ 173 612 | Public transport: service B5 links Mold with Loggerheads Country Park, about 3.2km (2 miles) from walk, Monday to Saturday; on Sundays and Bank Holiday Mondays the Clwydian Ranger buses serve both car parks met on this route (tel: 01824 706968) | Toilets: at car park | Nearest tourist information: Loggerheads Country Park

---

From the car park head to the large information board beside the stream and then take the path uphill into the trees, which is also

View from the Jubilee Tower towards the Dee Estuary

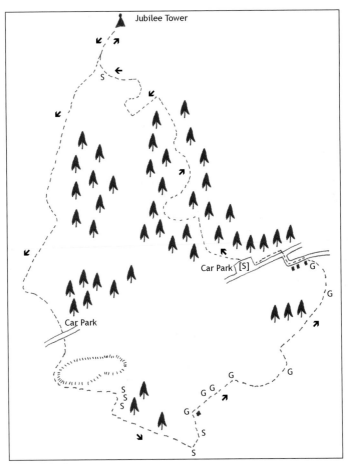

Map 1: Moel Famau

the start of several forest trails. Ignore the smaller paths to the nearby picnic tables and continue to climb to a junction with another path. Turn left on to this and continue climbing, then join a large forest track. Bear left on to this track, and where this forks bear left once more.

This track is flatter, but where it turns left, you should turn right on to a smaller path, back among the trees, and climb again. At a crossing track turn left and continue climbing. Stay on this main track as it passes a clearing on the left and then forks. Bear left on to a smaller path, into the clearing, with great views to your left. A small pond also becomes visible on the left. Follow the path as it bends round to the right and climbs again, before splitting once more. Bear right, as if heading back to the main track, but before you reach it the path veers round to the left again, gradually zigzagging its way uphill. If you need a breather, stop to look at the views behind you. The path then drops slightly, to a stile. Cross this and go through a gap in the stone wall to reach a wide track. Turn right and climb steeply, up to the remains of the Jubilee Tower with its astounding views.

After exploring the tower, return down the same wide track. When you reach the stile on your left, ignore this and continue ahead on the main track. There are excellent views to your right. This is the Offa's Dyke path. It drops steeply on a slate section and then, where it forks, bear right to stay on the wide track. After a gentle descent, the path forks once again. Bear right to remain on Offa's Dyke, signed with the acorn symbol, as it drops more steeply round to the left to reach another small car park.

Go through the car park and then cross over the lane and continue ahead on Offa's Dyke. Another steep climb is apparent. Follow the path as it zigzags its way halfway up the hill, before following the contour of the hill, around to the left. Follow the Offa's Dyke waymarks as the path climbs up through the remains of a fence and then around to the left in the ditch of an Iron Age hill fort earthwork. After another short, steep climb turn right, as signed, and follow the path along the contour of the hill once more, before dropping down to a stile. Cross this and then another one, to follow a path between some trees and a fence. Drop down to another stile into a field and follow the right-hand field edge, around the field as signed, until you reach a metal gate. Cross the

View over the Vale of Clwyd

stile by the side of this and continue to follow the tree line on your left. At the end of the field, turn left, off Offa's Dyke, over a stile by a metal gate on to a wide bridleway, downhill. This track then climbs up towards some farm buildings. Go through the wooden gate beside a metal one and bear right to continue climbing on this wide track. Proceed through two more gates in quick succession and continue along this wide track, which has good views to your right.

Follow the track through another large metal gate and continue as it bears round to the right and then the left. Continue through

another large metal gate. The bridleway now begins to drop downhill more noticeably and is joined by a track from your right. Ignore this and continue downhill, passing some confirmation waymarks on a wooden post on your left. There are excellent views over the Dee estuary from here. Continue downhill and go through a large metal gate before following the track around to the left. Drop down to another gate by a property, go through it and join a tarmac lane. Turn left to pass a couple of properties and follow the lane as it bears right and then climbs to join another lane. Take care as you cross over the lane and then cross the grass bank to reach a woodland path. Turn left and follow this all the way back to the car park.

POINTS OF INTEREST

▮ *Moel Famau means Mother's Mountain.*
▮ *The summit is 554m (1,818ft) above sea level.*
▮ *Within the country park are the remains of three Iron Age hill forts on the summits of Moel Fenlli, Moel y Gaer and Moel Arthur.*

OTHER WALKS IN THE AREA

There are several waymarked routes from this car park, and nearby Loggerheads Country Park has a range of walks exploring the industrial heritage of the area. Moel Arthur Iron Age hill fort is worth exploring.

WALK 2 | Llangollen

This is an energetic walk from the town centre to the summit of a 244m (800ft) hill where the remains of Castell Dinas Bran can be found. Although little of the castle remains today, the views from this, both up and down the Dee Valley, are amazing. The route then picks up Offa's Dyke to run along a quiet lane, marked on Ordnance Survey maps as Panorama Walk, before dropping down into the valley and following the level towpath of the Llangollen Canal back to the start.

This area has several links with the Scottish engineer Thomas Telford, who pushed what became the A5 route through the town towards Anglesey and who constructed the innovative Pontcysyllte, the aqueduct that carries the Llangollen Canal on 19 arches over the River Dee at a height of 38m (126ft). It can be glimpsed from various points along this route, as can the A5 through the Dee Valley.

Walk category: invigorating | Length: about 13km (8 miles) | Map: Explorer Sheet 256, Wrexham and Llangollen | Parking and starting point: there are several car parks in Llangollen Town Centre; start at Castle Street, Llangollen; grid ref: SJ 215 421 | Public transport: several services pass through Llangollen, mainly stopping at Market Street (tel: 01824 706800, Denbighshire Council, or visit www.denbighshire.gov.uk) | Toilets: at short-stay car park in Market Street and in Tourist Information Centre in Castle Street | Nearest tourist information: Llangollen

---

From any of the car parks or bus stops head for the main shopping thoroughfare in Llangollen, Castle Street, and continue

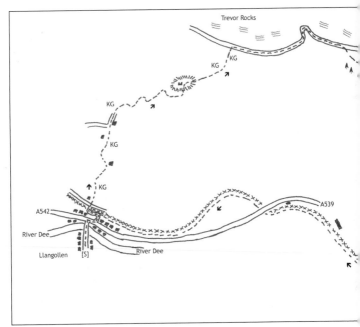

Map 2: Llangollen

over the bridge and across the River Dee and railway line. Turn
right briefly, before carefully crossing the main road and turning
left up Wharf Hill, which bends round to the left as it climbs up
towards the canal. Turn right to cross over the canal. At the road
junction in front of you cross over and head straight up some
steps to join a signed path. Climb gently, crossing over a metalled
track joining two sports facilities, and continue to climb up on a
path between fences.

Go through a kissing gate and cross straight over a lane, taking
the path, as signed, along the boundary on your right, which is
signed to the castle. Climb up the field edge, go through another
kissing gate and then continue ahead on a wide track. At a
junction of tracks cross straight over and continue climbing. Go

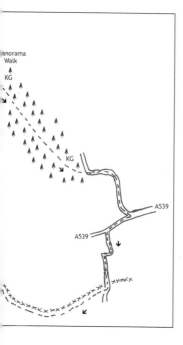

through another kissing gate to enter the Open Access area of Castle Dinas Bran.

Bear right and climb uphill to a level, grassy area with an information board. There are good views to be glimpsed from here and a hint of what's to come. Cross over the grassy area towards the castle, dropping briefly, before beginning the obvious zigzag route up to the castle summit. Take time to explore and enjoy the views.

When you are ready to move on, head for the opposite end of the castle from where you entered, drop down into a trench and then climb up over the rampart to reach a gently sloping turfed area. Head down this, looking out for a stone path where the drop becomes steeper. Follow this path as it bears around to the left, continuing its descent, to another kissing gate. Go through this, then zigzag down another obvious path. Follow it, as signed, around the right-hand side of a field, through some bushes to another kissing gate. Go through this to join a wide track. Turn left and shortly afterwards cross a cattle grid to join a single-track lane.

Turn right and follow this lane, which sees the occasional car, until you reach a turning on your right. Ignore this and bear left, uphill, with fine views across the Dee Valley on your right. The lane soon turns sharp left and then sharp right around a fold in the hill, before continuing a long, gentle climb. You may notice the signs for Offa's Dyke, because the walk follows this lane, too.

River Dee at Llangollen

Where the lane bears left once more, next to a car parking area, turn right, as signed, on to a wide track, which zigzags down briefly before straightening into a gentle descent. Just before a wooden gate marking the entrance to a private property turn right, as signed, and then drop down along a stone wall on your left. At a junction with another path, turn left to walk in front of the house and continue between two stone walls. Go through a kissing gate to enter the woods and shortly after pass through a much larger gate.

The path gently undulates through a mixture of coniferous and broadleaved trees. At a junction with a path turn left, as signed, and then shortly after another path joins from the left. Continue ahead in the same direction, where another path joins from the left, and then climb up on to a path with a field on your left. Run alongside the entire length of this field and at a junction bear right, downhill, to a kissing gate. Go through this and turn left on to a wide track.

When you reach a tarmac lane turn right and follow it round to the right, where it drops down to the main A539. Take care here

Panorama Walk and the Dee Valley

because this can be a busy road, but there is a tarmac path running alongside it. Turn right, away from the village of Trevor, and follow this downhill for a short way until you see a small, single-track lane on your left. Cross the A539 with care and go down this quiet lane, which passes under a disused railway bridge before meandering its way to the canal. Cross over the canal and then turn left to drop down to the towpath. Turn left again to go under bridge 34 and follow the towpath.

This takes you all the way back to Llangollen, but you may be surprised when you see how high the canal sits in the valley. At

numerous points there are glimpses of the River Dee down to your left. Stay on the towpath as it passes under bridges 35, 36, 37 and 38 and then under the wider bridge that used to carry the railway line. Continue under bridges 40 and 41, before travelling underneath the bridge that carries the A539 overhead.

After going under bridge 43, the towpath reaches the outskirts of Llangollen and becomes a tarmac path with mooring opportunities for canal boats. Continue alongside all of these, and once you have gone under bridge 45 turn left to rejoin Wharf Hill, which you may recognise from the start of the walk. Drop down

Wharf Hill to rejoin the A539 and turn left, then right, to cross over the railway and the River Dee to return to the centre of Llangollen.

POINTS OF INTEREST

■ *Dinas Bran translates into English as 'Crow City' or 'Crow Castle' and dates from the 13th century.*
■ *The Pontcysyllte, which stretches across the Dee Valley for about 307m (1,007ft), was completed in 1805.*
■ *The Llangollen Canal is 66km (41 miles) long and links up with the Shropshire Union Canal near Nantwich in Cheshire.*

OTHER WALKS IN THE AREA

Ruabon Mountain provides some fine walking opportunities with excellent views, as does the intriguingly named World's End. Alternatively, you can follow the Llangollen Canal further upstream and then pick up a path that will allow you to explore Valle Crucis Abbey, founded in 1201, before returning to Llangollen using the Clwydian Way.

Bangor-is-y-coed

Bangor-is-y-coed, or Bangor-on-Dee to give it its English name, is a quiet village on the banks of the River Dee in an area known locally as the Maelor. The English–Welsh border cuts into this very English landscape, which contrasts considerably from the more mountainous areas some 32.2km (20 miles) to the west. It's an area to be savoured slowly, and this short, gentle walk ambles around the banks of the Dee before circumnavigating its way around the east of the village, to finish up on the banks of the Dee beside a perfectly positioned public house.

Walk category: easy | Length: about 5km (3 miles) | Map: Explorer Sheet 257, Crewe and Nantwich | Parking and starting point: park near church, opposite Royal Oak pub; grid ref: SJ 389 455 | Public transport: service 146 (Whitchurch–Wrexham), Monday to Saturday (tel: 01978 266166, Wrexham Bus Line) | Toilets: none | Nearest tourist information: Wrexham

Park considerately near to St Dunawd Church in Bangor-on-Dee, opposite the Royal Oak pub, and head towards the river. Cross over the road and turn right down a track that leads between the Royal Oak and the river, passing a boathouse on your left. Go through a large metal gate and continue on the path, as signed, to reach another gate. Go through this to remain on the track, which bears left where the earth flood barrier bears away to the right. At the next fence bear left to go through the kissing gate and follow the path as it now travels along the riverbank.

Continue around to the next fence line, go through another kissing gate and remain along the bank side. After passing through

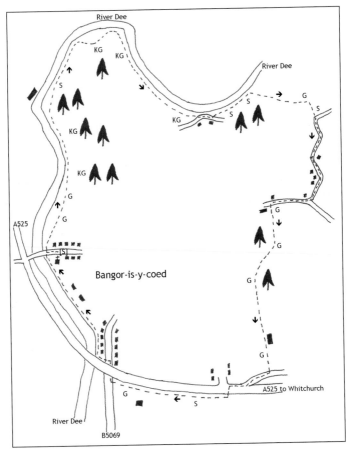

Map 3: Bangor-is-y-coed

the next tree line, the path now begins to bear right as the River Dee turns in this direction. Cross over a stile and stay on this path. Soon the river turns to the right and the main path heads towards a fence, but bear right away from the obvious path to follow a fence line on the left. Then take the kissing gate in that fence to go through into the next field. Head back towards the riverbank and follow it round to the next kissing gate. Go through this, and bear right, away from the river, under the pylons and towards a set of steps with a handrail up to the top of the earth flood defence. Climb up these, then drop down the other side and go through the kissing gate ahead, to the left of a large metal gate.

Turn left on to a tarmac lane and shortly after take the next set of steps on your left, back up on to the flood defence earth bank, and turn right to follow the top. Head into some trees and cross over a stile and continue to the next stile. Cross this and then take the steps on the left. Bear away from the river, to head towards the bridge that allows you to pass under the disused railway embankment. Go through the gate and then, on the other side, turn right to follow the embankment along the field edge to a stile on the right of a metal gate. Cross this and at a tarmac lane continue straight ahead.

Follow this lane as it meanders through the quiet countryside, eventually passing some dwellings before climbing up to a junction with a road. Turn right and take care as you follow this road over a bridge across a disused railway. Pick up the narrow tarmac pedestrian path on the right. Stay on this until just before you re-enter the village of Bangor-is-coed, where you should cross over the road to take the signed bridleway on your left. Go through the gate and follow the left-hand field edge to the next field corner. Pass through the gate in the hedge and then bear right, diagonally across the next field, to a similar gate in the opposite hedge. Continue through this, then follow the left-hand field boundary in front of Highgate House and around to a large gate on the left.

Go through this gate and turn right to follow the driveway to a slip road. Turn right on to the tarmac pedestrian path and follow this slip road downhill to meet the main A525. Continue ahead towards the road junction on the right signed to Bangor-is-y-coed.

Bridge over the River Dee

Opposite this junction is a signed path, so cross the A525 carefully, then turn left, as signed, behind the traffic signs and drop down on a narrow path. This soon levels and passes a field on your left. Cross over a stile and continue ahead to reach a large metal gate. Go through this to meet the B5069 and turn right, under the A525, then cross the road to turn left and take the steps that lead up to another path beside the river. Turn right and follow this back towards the church, where the path bears right between the war memorial and the church to return to the road.

POINTS OF INTEREST

- *Bangor-is-y-coed was once the site of a Celtic Christian monastery, with over 3,000 monks.*

- *The 17th-century sandstone bridge across the River Dee was built by Inigo Jones, the first Englishman to study architecture in Italy.*
- *Bangor-is-y-coed translates as 'Bangor below the Wood'.*

OTHER WALKS IN THE AREA

An information board by the church gives details of other walks, including a circular route to the village of Worthenbury, and routes along the other side of the river. A leaflet is also available from the tourist information centre.

| Ceiriog Valley

Chocoholics will either love or hate this walk. The large Cadbury's factory at Chirk produces a lovely chocolatey aroma that fills the air, and wafts of the scent will assail your nostrils at various sections of the route depending on the direction of the wind. It should also be noted that this walk uses permissive routes across the National Trust property of Chirk Castle that are open only between 1 April and 30 September. At other times of the year you will have to take a road detour around the park, but the route is obvious on the Ordnance Survey map. This walk provides a perfect opportunity to explore Chirk Castle, the only fortress built during the reign of Edward I that is still lived in today, with views over nine counties. To check opening times visit www.nationaltrust.org.uk.

The walk then drops down into the Ceiriog Valley, once an important route from England into the Snowdonia region of Wales, hence the construction of Chirk Castle. It's a quiet valley these days, but one that Lloyd George described as 'a little bit of heaven on Earth'. Not only does this walk explore both the English and Welsh sides of the Ceiriog Valley, but it also takes a trip across Thomas Telford's Chirk aqueduct, which runs 21m (70ft) across the valley floor.

Walk category: moderate | Length: about 12km (7½ miles) | Map: Explorer Sheet 240, Oswestry | Parking and starting point: main car park in Chirk; grid ref: SJ 291 378 | Public transport: Wrexham Bus Line services through Chirk (tel: 01978 266166) | Toilets: at car park, Chirk, and at Home Farm visitor centre, Chirk Castle | Nearest tourist information: Wrexham

Boats on Llangollen Canal

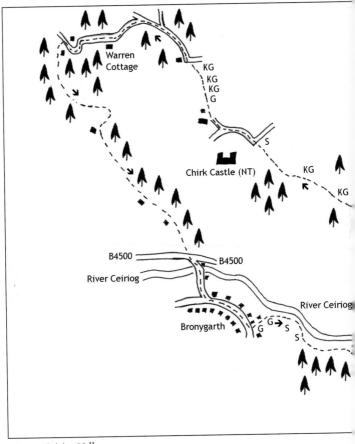

Map 4: Ceiriog Valley

From the main car park return to Colliery Road and turn left to meet the main road. Turn left again, passing Hand Terrace on your left. Cross over the road to take Station Avenue on your right, beside the war memorial, and follow this for its entire length, passing the Cadbury factory on your right a little later on. At a junction continue ahead over the railway bridge, passing the railway station on your right, before the entrance to a small industrial park on your right.

Shortly after the Llangollen branch of the Shropshire Union Canal emerges from a tunnel on your right, take the next signed footpath on your right, into the trees and on to a broad track. The canal remains in a cutting on your right, but watch out for a waymark, signing the path up some steps on the left on to a bank, before dropping down to a kissing gate on the left. Go through this and then head across the field to the kissing gate on the other side.

Go through the gate and turn right on to the lane. (If you are tackling this walk between 1 October and 31 March skirt around the estate by staying on the tarmac lane for 2km (1¼ miles) and then taking the next lane on the left at a crossroads.) Between 1 April and 30 September you can turn left up a track to a kissing gate on the left of a metal gate to join the permissive footpath across the Chirk estate. Go through the kissing gate and head into the field, keeping the boundary fence on your left. Take care because there may be livestock in these fields. Continue towards another kissing gate beside a metal gate, go through and then

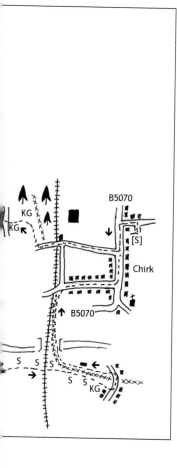

Walkers in Ceiriog Valley

bear right, aiming for a white-topped post. Once past this, continue between some trees towards another kissing gate in the corner of the field, marked by another post. Go through this and bear left, keeping along the metal fence and bearing right slightly where marked by another marker post, with a small copse on your left. Continue down towards a stile by a small metal gate. Cross over the stile to join the driveway that skirts around Chirk Castle on your left. Take care because cars entering the park use this driveway during opening hours, but the grass verges are wide enough to use safely.

Follow the driveway round to the car park and bear right to pass Home Farm visitor centre on your left. During opening hours there are toilets and a shop here, and if you have time Chirk Castle is worth a visit. Follow the track that lies between a fence on the left and the car park on the right, go over a cattle grid and then climb gently to a wooden gate. Go through and continue ahead to a kissing gate next to a larger gate. Pass through this and continue climbing gently, keeping with the field boundary on your left. Again, note that there may be livestock in these fields. The route then continues through two more kissing gates to join a tarmac lane by a couple of properties on the left. (Those who are using the lane route instead of the permissive path route will rejoin this walk at this point.)

Continue ahead on this lane as it climbs, ignoring the path on your left. The route becomes steep here, but this is the steepest section and is only short. Where the lane forks, bear left on to a narrower lane, and then when this forks bear left again, passing a waymark on the left signed as the Llwyber Ceiriog Trail.

Drop downhill, passing Warren Cottage on your left and later ignoring another signed footpath on the left. The path falls steeply, and you should veer right as the lane passes another cottage on the right, and then turn sharp left, as signed, to stay on the trail, continuing downhill and passing another cottage on your right. Soon you reach a fork by a cottage on the left. Bear left to climb gently.

The path continues through the trees, offering glimpses to your right of the Ceiriog Valley. At a junction with a crossing track, bear right to drop downhill. Offa's Dyke National Trail soon joins from the left, but follow the track as it bears right downhill and becomes a tarmac track. Continue through a farm, dropping further and passing another cottage on your right. When you reach a junction, bear left, as signed, where the route climbs briefly to a fork. Here you should bear right, as signed, to drop down to the B4500.

Take care as you cross straight over the road to stay on Offa's Dyke and continue on a quiet lane over the River Ceiriog. Welcome to England. This lane continues to climb up to reach a junction with another lane. Turn left, signed as the Maelor Way, and follow this quiet road towards the picturesque village of Bronygarth. Look out for some disused lime kilns on the right. As the lane climbs gently there are some good views across the valley to Chirk Castle on the other side. Continue through Bronygarth and after the Old School on your right take the next signed path on your left. This drops downhill, and at a crossing track continue straight over, as signed, down to two gates. Go through both of these to continue on a path between two fences.

Drop down to cross a stile by a gate, bearing right, as signed, to another stile. Cross this and enter Pentre Wood. Follow the track through the trees, bearing right where signed and up some steps, before dropping down more steps to a junction. Turn right to drop down further steps to a path that runs close to the riverside. Ignore the path where it turns right, but continue ahead over a ditch and then cross a stile to enter a field. Continue along the riverbank and you may notice the private fishing pools on the other side of the river. The path becomes a wide track as it meanders through an embankment into another field, with houses on your right. Continue round to reach a stile by a metal gate.

Cross over this stile and continue ahead on a quiet tarmac lane until you reach a junction with another lane. Turn right and climb uphill, taking the next lane on the left. This passes some dwellings on the left, and you may capture glimpses of the viaduct and aqueduct further down the valley. Before the lane turns sharp right, bear left on to a path that is level to begin with, before it gently climbs up to a stile. Cross this to enter a field. Follow the boundary fence to another stile. Cross this and stay along the left-hand field boundary to reach the railway line. Take extreme care here. Cross over a stile and drop down the steps to reach the railway line. Cross over if clear, climb up the concrete steps and cross another stile. Bear right to follow the left-hand boundary of the field, with the canal down to your left.

At the end of the field, cross a stile, continue over a track, then another stile and follow the path between two fences. Drop down to a kissing gate, and then turn left on to a pedestrian path along a residential road. Follow this downhill and cross over the canal. Turn left on to a wide tarmac lane, which runs alongside the canal, passing a few properties on your right. Eventually this lane narrows to a path as the canal turns right to cross the valley. Follow the towpath across the aqueduct, with the viaduct above you on the left. At the other side of the valley you re-enter Wales.

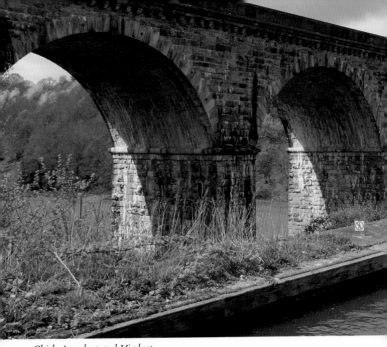

Chirk Aqueduct and Viaduct

Bear right, to follow the main path, signed towards the town centre. At the top, cross over the road and turn right to use the pedestrian path back to Chirk. Continue over the mini-roundabout, and when you reach the junction with the main B5070, turn left to return to the war memorial at Station Avenue. Turn right to cross over the main road and return to the car park.

POINTS OF INTEREST

■ *Lloyd George is the only Welshman to have held the office as British prime minister.*

■ *Chirk aqueduct was built between 1796 and 1801 by Thomas Telford and William Jessop. The aqueduct cost £20,898 to build and stretches*

for 216m (710ft) across the valley. The viaduct is 9m (30ft) higher than the aqueduct.

OTHER WALKS IN THE AREA

Bus connections between Chirk and Oswestry make it possible to do a linear walk along Offa's Dyke between the two towns. Some of the best sections of the original earth dyke can be seen along this section. The Ceiriog Trail explores the more isolated western end of the Ceiriog Valley.

The area around Ellesmere is often referred to as Shropshire's Lake District, although the nine meres (lakes) are considerably smaller than those in Cumbria. Only a few are accessible to the public, and this walk uses the Llangollen Canal to link a short section of The Mere at Ellesmere with a circuitous route around Cole Mere. For the adventurous, the Llangollen Canal travels under the junction of the A528 and A495 through an 80m (262ft) tunnel. The towpath along the canal inside the tunnel is quite restricted for height and gets dark in the middle. You might want to pack a torch for this route. Alternatively, you can go over the top, although this does mean taking great care as you negotiate the road junction.

Cole Mere is a designated local nature reserve, and it is also a Site of Special Scientific Interest and a RAMSAR site (a world designated wetland area). You might be able to spot curlew, pochard and goldeneye swimming on the water, as well as southern marsh orchids and lady's smock flowering in the adjoining meadow.

This walk, which follows mainly canal towpaths and lakeside shores, is relatively level and easy to walk.

Walk category: moderate | Length: about 10km (6¼ miles) | Map: Explorer Sheet 241, Shrewsbury, Wem, Shawbury and Baschurch | Parking and starting point: Castlefields car park, off A495, near The Mere, Ellesmere; grid ref: SJ 407 345 | Public transport: Arriva Midlands North service 501 (Shrewsbury–Ellesmere), weekdays (tel: 01543 466123) | Toilets: opposite car park | Nearest tourist information: Ellesmere

---

Blakemere

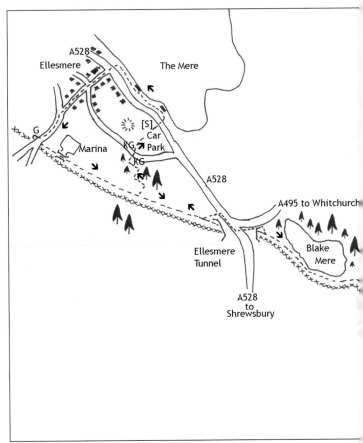

Map 5: Ellesmere

From the Castlefields car park drop back down to the main A528 and cross with care. Turn left on to the pedestrian path, and you will soon pass the toilets on your right, followed shortly after by the Boathouse tea gardens and coffee shop and the Meres visitor centre.

Walk along the shoreline of The Mere. This is a popular area with tourists, and the water is usually packed with ducks and geese, eager for any handouts of food. Continue until you reach the entrance to Cremorne Gardens. Do not enter but instead follow the pedestrian path uphill, away from The Mere and into town. Take care because the path is narrow here. Turn left to cross over the A528, and take the small lane, Church Hill, between Ellesmere House on your left and the church on your right. Continue climbing gently until you reach a junction. Bear left and then almost immediately bear right on to a smaller lane, which drops gently, between two high walls. At a junction with a wider road, cross over carefully to reach a tarmac path and then turn left.

Follow this round to your right, passing a marina on the left, before climbing up to a bridge over the canal. Don't cross the bridge, but turn right through a gate to drop down to the canal towpath. Turn left and follow the towpath under the bridge. Soon after, bear left to continue on the towpath as it crosses the link between the canal and the marina.

Continue along here, ignoring the signed path on the left to the visitor centre and Castle Mound, and about 400m (¼ mile) further on there is another footpath on the left, signed to the

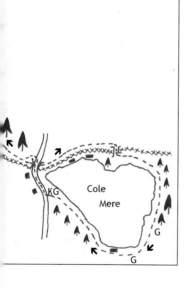

The Mere at Ellesmere

Moors car park. Ignore this as well and follow the towpath, signed to Cole Mere. Ahead is the Ellesmere Tunnel, which is 80m (262ft) long. The towpath does pass through the tunnel, although it is narrow and has little headroom. The route of this walk follows this, but if you do not feel comfortable about tackling the tunnel, bear left where the path forks and climb up

to the main road. (Walkers using the tunnel should continue ahead through it.) This is a busy junction and extreme care should be taken. Cross over the junction of the A528 and the A495 Whitchurch road, using the small islands in the road. Cross over to reach a car park, turn left to reach its entrance and then turn right into it. From here, you will see a wooden waymark pointing to a path on your left signed for Cole Mere. Take this as it drops back down to the towpath, where you will meet any walkers who have used the tunnel.

Soon the towpath bears around to the right. Follow this with the canal on your right and Blake Mere on your left. The towpath proceeds around the bottom edge of the mere, turning left, before bearing around to the right once more. Stay on this as it continues under a small bridge and, once you are under a second bridge, you will catch glimpses of Cole Mere on your right.

The canal and Cole Mere are both on your right, so continue along the towpath to the next bridge. Go under it and once through, bear left to climb up some steps to cross over the bridge. At the other side, turn left on to another path so that the canal is now on your left. Soon this path bears right, away from the canal, and drops down some steps on to a good path into the trees. Follow this as it gently meanders around to the right, reaching a small bridge over a stream immediately before a wooden gate.

Go through the gate and turn right on to a wooden boardwalk section, which leads to, and then follows, the shoreline of Cole Mere on your right. Continue ahead on to a grassy section to reach another wooden gate. Go through, and turn right to follow the boundary fence of the sailing club, and at a junction with a wide track bear left, as signed, to continue towards a boathouse. Soon after, you enter Boathouse Wood. Follow this wide path along the water's edge.

Ignore any sidetracks and remain on this path until you reach a kissing gate beside a large wooden gate. Go through and turn right on to a narrow lane, passing some dwellings on your left. Climb up to the canal bridge, cross over and then turn right to drop down some steps to the towpath once more. Turn right to go under the bridge and begin the return journey back along the canal side.

Stay on the towpath, passing Blake Mere once again, and negotiating the tunnel by using either the towpath that runs through it or the busy road junction above. Follow the towpath. Ignore the first signed path on your right to the Moors car park and continue the 400m (¼ mile) to the next turning on your right, signed to the visitor centre and Castle Mound.

Turn right on to this permissive path between fences, zigzagging up to the Shropshire Wildlife Trust nature reserve. Cross over a small wooden bridge. Ignoring the small track on your right, continue to follow the hedge line on your left. At the next junction turn right, as signed, uphill into the trees, and at the top turn left, as signed, to continue climbing, before dropping down some steps to a wooden kissing gate.

Go through this and cross the lane to pass through another wooden kissing gate, bearing right to return to the car park.

POINTS OF INTEREST

- *The meres are remnants of the Ice Age and were created under the weight of the ice, which melted into them. Blake Mere was created over 12,000 years ago.*
- *Cole Mere was bought by Shropshire County Council in the early 1970s and became the county's first country park.*
- *The word mere is derived from the Anglo-Saxon word for lake. However, the water levels of lakes are maintained by streams flowing into and out of them, whereas the meres are supplied through drainage from the surrounding area.*

OTHER WALKS IN THE AREA

Footpaths connect the canal with local villages, providing longer routes around Ellesmere and Welshampton, returning to Ellesmere via the Llangollen Canal.

| Pistyll Rhaeadr

Size isn't everything, but in this walk it certainly makes a difference. Pistyll Rhaeadr is a spectacular waterfall, formed where the River Rhaeadr plummets 73m (240ft) into the valley below. It's an isolated tourist spot, and the tea room situated at its foot is perfectly positioned for the best view. However, it's also a good starting point from which to conquer Cadair Berwyn, at 830m (2,723ft) the highest point in the Berwyn Mountains round here. On a clear day it is possible to see west to Snowdonia and east to England.

Walk category: moderate | *Length: about 9km (5½ miles)* | *Map: Explorer Sheet 255, Llangollen and Berwyn* | *Parking and starting point: car park at tea rooms at Pistyll Rhaeadr, small charge; grid ref: SJ 074 295* | *Public transport: none; the car park is reached by a 6.4km (4 mile) single-track road* | *Toilets: at car park* | *Nearest tourist information: Lake Vyrnwy*

From the car park walk back towards the road. Immediately on your left, after the entrance, take the path that climbs up. Ignore the gate on the left and continue between some stone walls and bear left through a wooden gate, turning right, as signed. Continue through a kissing gate to enter Open Access land and follow this path until it forks. Bear right on to a wide track that climbs gently, and then bear left to enter the left-hand side of a valley. Where this track turns sharp left, turn right on to a grassy path, which drops down to a stream. Cross this, and then continue over a stile and follow the path up to a junction with a wide track.

Pistyll Rhaeadr waterfall

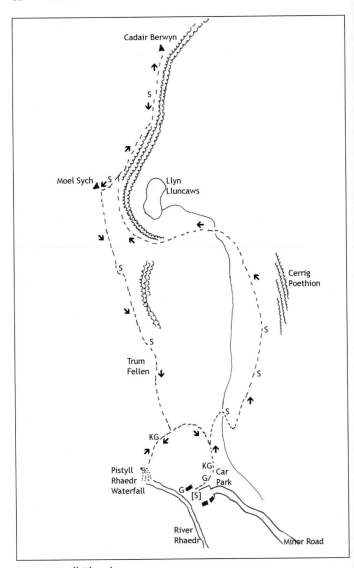

Map 6: Pistyll Rhaeadr

Turn sharp left to follow this track along the right-hand side of the valley. Climb steadily, up to a stile, cross over and continue to another stile. Continue over this and follow this path as the valley gradually narrows and the ground becomes boggier. Eventually, the path crosses through the stream and continues climbing upwards, passing a waymark denoting the start of a permissive path to the summit of Cadair Berwyn.

This meanders gently left, before crossing another small stream and continuing to climb. You might find it becoming boggier underfoot as it skirts around the left-hand edge of Llyn Lluncaws, before bearing left again to begin a steeper climb.

The path pushes upwards and to the right of a rocky outcrop, where it then begins to bear right and follow the edge of the escarpment. Take care, as the path hogs the edge closely. Listen out for peregrine falcons that may be heard calling. The cliff ledges are ideal nesting and perching sites.

Soon the path begins to level as it reaches the top of the escarpment, and views to the east and west open up. Bear left towards the boundary fence and continue ahead. Cross over the ladder stile to reach the highest section of this route, sometimes referred to as Cadair Berwyn New Top, as it is 3m (10ft) higher than Cadair Berwyn, with the triangulation point on its summit. Continue over the highest point then drop down, passing a small pool on your left before climbing to the trig point to mark the 827m (2,713ft) of Cadair Berwyn. There are excellent views from here across North Wales.

Ignore the ladder stile. Turn around and return using the same path, over the highest point, to reach the ladder stile. Once you've climbed over, keep the boundary fence close on the right and continue ahead, dropping down at first, before climbing again. Ignore the path on the left, used during the ascent, and continue along the fence until you reach another ladder stile. Cross this and continue to the large cairn, which marks the summit of Moel Sych.

Moel Sych and Cadair Berwyn

Turn left here and follow a permissive path back down to Pistyll Rhaeadr (as was signed on the ladder stile). The path is quite boggy again as it drops steeply, before becoming stonier and easier to walk on. Look out for another ladder stile on your left. Cross this, turning right to continue downhill, with the fence now on your right. The path becomes boggy once more, then climbs briefly, before descending quite steeply in places to reach another ladder stile.

Cross this stile and bear left slightly, as signed, to follow the path as it drops downhill, towards the left-hand side of the adja-

cent valley. Make sure that you bear left and follow the path around the right-hand side of a rocky outcrop on your left, to begin a steeper descent. Soon, the path crosses over a ditch. Continue downhill towards a kissing gate in a stone wall, but stop when you reach a wide crossing track.

To visit the top of the Pistyll Rhaeadr waterfall continue over this crossing track, drop down to the kissing gate, go through it and follow the path to the stream. Note that there are no handrails or barriers at the water's edge. Return the same way to reach the crossing track and turn right.

If you don't want to visit the top of the waterfall, turn left on to this wide track, which climbs briefly and bears left, before dropping. Turn right, as signed, on to a path that zigzags steeply down the hill, using steps in places and turning right again at a junction. Follow this path through the kissing gate to return to the car park.

To explore the bottom of the waterfall, take the small gate to the right of the entrance to the tea room, and a short path will take you to a good vantage point.

POINTS OF INTEREST

▪ *Pistyll Rhaeadr's drop from top to bottom is 73m (240ft), which is 18m (60ft) higher than Niagara Falls. Pistyll Rhaeadr was the 1,000th Site of Special Scientific Interest (SSSI) to be designated in Wales.*
▪ *In 1974 it was alleged that the Berwyn Mountains were the crash site of a UFO.*

OTHER WALKS IN THE AREA

This walk could be extended to include Cadair Bronwem, a further 2km (1¼ miles) from Cadair Berwyn, while several footpaths around the foot of the waterfall allow the southern shores of the Afon Rhaeadr, with its historical mine workings, to be explored.

This walk is proof that you don't need to climb mountains to see fine views. Corbett Wood is owned by Shropshire County Council, which provides the car parking facilities, although Grinshill Hill is in private ownership. Access is permitted, however, although any notices restricting access should be adhered to at all times. Grinshill Hill stone has been quarried extensively, and much of it is in use around Shropshire. As a result, there are some nasty drops around, but conversely, some spectacular views over southern Shropshire, mid-Wales, Staffordshire and the Cheshire plain. Eagle-eyed walkers may even be able to pick out Jodrell Bank. This short walk offers rewarding views for little effort.

Walk category: easy | Length: about 5km (3 miles) | Map: Explorer Sheet 241, Shrewsbury | Parking and starting point: Corbet Wood picnic site; grid ref: SJ 525 238 | Public transport: Arriva Midlands North services 511 and 513 serve Grinshill and Clive (tel: 01543 466123) | Toilets: none | Nearest tourist information: Shrewsbury

---

Turn around to face the car park entrance and begin to walk towards it, but before you reach the building on the right, turn right, next to a litter bin, and follow this path. Fork around to the right, so that you continue to follow the path as it sinks between steep banks and negotiates its way around the car park, into a sunken ditch, before it briefly opens up again. The path follows a wooden fence on the left, and then drops down between banks once more to reach a large junction of tracks.

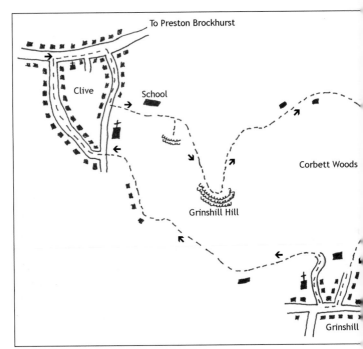

Map 7: Grinshill

Turn sharp left and immediately fork left, to pick up a path that gently drops down through Corbett Woods. Where the path forks, bear right, and then right again at another junction, on to a wide, sandy bridleway. Between the trees you may catch glimpses of the south Shropshire hills on the left. Watch out for the quarries on your right, accessible with care through the trees.

Stay on this path as it bears around to the left, joining with the Shropshire Way long-distance path. Bear left and follow this between the banks. Where the path forks, bear left to join a wide track that joins from the right. Continue along this track between buildings and tennis courts into Grinshill. At the junction with the road, turn right.

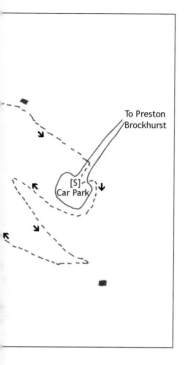

To Preston
Brockhurst

[S]-
Car Park

Soon after joining the road, take the next right, a signed footpath, which passes the Victorian All Saints Church in Grinshill. Continue along this track, between the houses, and where it bears right towards the village hall fork left behind a property and continue through a sunken section of this lane. Ignore any side turnings, and follow this wide track as views open up again on the left. Continue around the bottom of Grinshill Hill and eventually the path begins to climb, passing several small dwellings, before bearing left to drop down past the church in the village of Clive.

At the junction with the road, continue straight over, as if going to Clive village club, and then bear right, following the road through this quiet village, until you reach another road junction. Turn right, passing the village stores and post office on your left. Ignore the first road on your right, but take the second, which is called Drawwell and which leads back up to the church. At the church lich-gate turn left on to a wide stone path that climbs gently. Ignore the drive on your left and continue on this main track until you reach Clive primary school on your left. A brief diversion to your right will reward you with great views on a clear day.

From the school continue in the same upward direction, and where the path forks bear right to climb up on to the privately

View from Grinshill Hill towards the Breidden Hills

owned Grinshill Hill, passing a 'welcome' sign on your left. Follow this obvious track as it climbs gently towards the summit, where a beacon on a large pole is permanently lit as a warning to the helicopter pilots from nearby RAF Shawbury. Take extreme care here because there are no barriers at the cliff edges. The views extend almost 360 degrees, across Shropshire, Cheshire, Staffordshire and Wales.

Turn around, so that the cliff and beacon are behind you, and take the grassy path directly ahead. This soon becomes an

earthy path through the trees and bracken, with a glimpse of Clive church to your left. Follow this as it bears left through the trees and then drops down to a wide track by a metal gate. Turn right and follow this track, with open fields and extensive views again on your left. Follow this track past dwellings on both sides, and at a signed crossroads continue straight ahead. Follow this until you reach a tarmac lane opposite the entrance to some quarry works. Turn right to return to the car park.

POINTS OF INTEREST

- *Stone from the Grinshill quarries can be found in Shrewsbury's market hall and on the façade of Shrewsbury railway station.*
- *Grinshill Hill is one of the highest points in north Shropshire yet is only 192m (630ft) above sea level.*
- *Clive church is one of the few churches in Shropshire to have a spire.*

OTHER WALKS IN THE AREA

Both the Shropshire Way and the Marches Way intersect here, providing further opportunities for exploring the locality by using some of the quieter roads to create a circular route.

WALK 8 | Lake Vyrnwy

The village of Llanwddyn paid the price for Liverpool's water supply when the valley was flooded to create Lake Vyrnwy. It had to be razed to the ground and rebuilt on the eastern side of the dam, which was constructed in 1881–9. The 7.6km (4¾ mile) long reservoir it created looks magical when it is bathed in sunshine and the blue skies are reflected in its surface, and the turreted straining tower along its northeastern shore adds further enchantment. Despite being just 35km (22 miles) from the border town of Oswestry, Lake Vyrnwy nestles on the outskirts of the Berwyn Mountains, and the boundary of its northwestern catchment area nudges against the boundary of the Snowdonia National Park.

This glorious setting makes a circumnavigation of the reservoir an enjoyable walk. Categorised as 'invigorating' because of its length, it is actually a level stroll along the tarmac road that follows the shoreline. Take care when you are using this road, particularly at weekends and on bank holidays, because it is popular with drivers. However, the traffic doesn't detract from the walk, because the road is relatively narrow, forcing drivers to take it steadily, especially when the route is busy with walkers, runners and cyclists.

Walking around the reservoir also gives opportunities to stop and explore, which drivers can do only at designated car parks. So take time to saunter around and enjoy the views from one side of the reservoir, before crossing over and seeing the views on the other side.

Walk category: invigorating | *Length: about 18.5km (11½ miles)* | *Map: Explorer Sheet 239, Lake Vyrnwy and Llanfyllin* | *Parking and starting point: main car park at Lake Vyrnwy visitor centre; grid ref: SJ 019 190* | *Public transport: none* | *Toilets: next to dam* | *Nearest tourist information: Lake Vyrnwy*

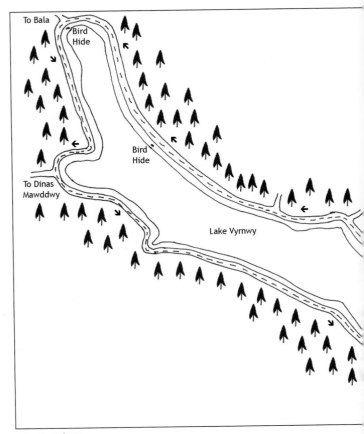

Map 8: Lake Vyrnwy

From the main car park, take the stepped path, signed to the visitor centre, and when you reach the narrow road turn right to continue on a path that passes a coffee shop on the right and the RSPB visitor centre on the left. When you reach the dam, there are toilets on the left. Turn right to cross over the dam, taking time to explore the information panels in several of the bays that explain the history of the reservoir and the dam. When you reach the other side, look out for the commemorative plaques.

Turn left on to the road and follow this along the edge of the reservoir, where the straining tower can be glimpsed through the trees. Follow this around to the left, passing the entrance to the Lake Vyrnwy Hotel, and cross over a stone bridge. Look for a commemorative tree on the right, planted in 1910 by the then Prince of Wales to mark the final opening of the reservoir. The road bears right, and soon you'll see the Victorian architecture of the straining tower at closer quarters. Continue along the road, passing a private road on the right, and shortly after there is an opportunity to get closer to the water's edge. If you wish, you can take the gravel path on your left into the trees, which meanders closer to the reservoir, crossing a wooden bridge,

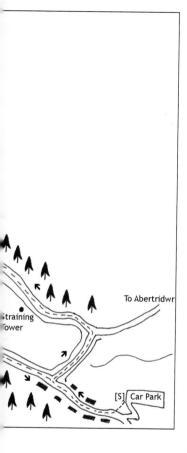

To Abertridwr

Straining Tower

[S] Car Park

before veering sharp right, back up to the road once more. Turn left to rejoin the road and pass a picnic spot on your left, where there are fine views across the reservoir.

The road now bears left over another bridge, crossing the River Cedig as it plummets to the water, and passes a road on the right signed to the Lakeview tea rooms. The road then narrows, but the verge is wide enough in most places to step on so that you can

Looking along Lake Vyrnwy

avoid passing cars, although it is a little too soft to walk on all the time. After wandering alongside some grazing fields on the right, the road re-enters the trees and begins its gentle arc to the right to the upper reaches of the reservoir. A good place for a rest is the Lakeside bird hide on the left, a wooden hide right on the water's edge, which provides an opportunity see a wide range of wild

birds throughout the year, including teal, pochard, great crested grebes and even kingfishers.

When the road reaches the grassy end of the reservoir, it bears left, passing the path to Rhiwargor bird hide on the left and, shortly after, the single-track mountain road to Bala on the right. Follow the road through the coniferous trees as it begins the return leg to the dam along the southwestern shores of the reservoir. Continue over another bridge and pass a car park on the right, before following a relatively straight section of the road for about 1.6km (1 mile).

When the road bends sharp right, views stretching down the reservoir to the straining tower can be glimpsed through the trees. Stay on the road as it then bears left, passing another single-track mountain road, signed to Dinas Mawddwy on the right. Then cross another bridge over the River Eunant. Watch out for several waterfalls on the right as the valley walls on this side of the reservoir are steeper, forcing the water to race down towards the reservoir. Further breaks in the trees on the left offer more views up and down the reservoir.

Soon the road bears right to pass the Hafod car park on the left, before turning sharp left over another bridge, which crosses the River Hirddu. More waterfalls can be glimpsed along this section, and there is one in particular where a bridge carries the road over the bottom of the fall.

Another car park and picnic site appear on the left, offering good views across to the straining tower. It's a lovely spot to rest for a few minutes, before the final section of the walk back to the dam. Continue along this part of the road, where there are several viewpoints as it meanders along the water's edge, before passing the boat house car park on the left, from which there are good views of the dam. Follow the road back towards the dam, passing the RSPB visitor centre once again, to return to the car park.

POINTS OF INTEREST

▌ *Lake Vyrnwy is 800m (½ mile) wide at its widest point and has a maximum depth of 26m (84ft). It is capable of holding over 59,100 million litres (13,000 million gallons) of water. The dam is 39m (127ft) thick at its base and 357m (1,172ft) long, and it cost £620,000 to build.*

■ *The large straining tower or valve tower was designed by the architect George Frederick Deacon.*

OTHER WALKS IN THE AREA

The long-distance path Glyndwr's Way travels through the area on its route from Knighton to Welshpool, via Machynlleth, and the less well-known Pererindod Melangell Walk stretches for 24km (15 miles), linking the Vyrnwy and Tanat Valleys.

The Criggion estate, which owns much of this land, leases it to the Forestry Commission, and this means that much of it is private property. However, the estate has kindly created a couple of permissive footpaths, which this walk makes use of. Bear in mind that permissive paths can be closed at any time, and, particularly during the winter months, the permissive path on this route may be closed one day every week.

The target of this walk is Rodney's Pillar, which stands majestically on the summit of Breidden Hill. The views from here on a clear day include most of north Shropshire, the Severn Valley, The Wrekin and the south Shropshire hills as well as some of the Berwyn Mountains. The pillar was built to celebrate the victories of Admiral George Rodney over the French in the West Indies between 1780 and 1782. The reason it was built here, far from the sea, was because Rodney's boats were built from wood grown in the nearby Montgomeryshire forests. Trees were felled and then floated down the River Severn to the docks at Bristol, where they were used to construct his battle-winning warships.

Walk category: moderate | Length: about 5km (3 miles) | Map: Explorer Sheet 240, Oswestry, Chirk and Ellesmere | Parking and starting point: Forest Enterprise car park; grid ref: SJ 296 150 | Public transport: none, although services between Shrewsbury and Welshpool stop at Middletown on the other side of the Breidden Hills | Toilets: none | Nearest tourist information: Welshpool

Rodney's Pillar and Toposcope

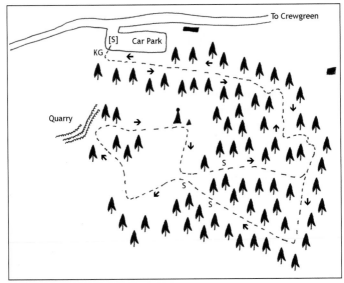

Map 9: Breidden Hills

From the Forest Enterprise car park climb up to the kissing gate on the right of the information panel, and then turn left on to the wide forest track. This is a permissive path and the one that is closed at various times throughout the year. Follow this as it gently climbs through the trees, zigzagging to reach a bridleway that joins from the left. Stay on this track briefly, and then turn right on to the signed bridleway that climbs steeply up into the trees. Where the bridleway appears to fork, stay on the left to climb up to a junction. Turn left to remain on the bridleway, which continues to climb, and as it gains altitude the views over north Shropshire and the Welsh borders towards Oswestry become ever more impressive. Soon the bridleway levels out. At a junction turn right on to a signed path. Another small track soon joins from the left, but continue heading in the same direction towards Rodney's Pillar, which you may be able to glimpse in front of you.

Continue to ignore any smaller tracks until you reach a stile. Cross this and turn right to follow the path around to another stile beside a wide grass path. Cross this stile and turn left. The path soon begins to drop, offering views towards Welshpool. When you reach an obvious crossing track turn right on to a signed bridleway and follow this uphill, through a stone wall and eventually breaking free of the tree line. Stay on this path as it bends sharp right, as signed, on to the open hillside. Take extreme care with any young children or dogs here because of the quarry on the left. There are plenty of warning signs.

The bridleway makes its final ascent towards Rodney's Pillar, but look out for the toposcope on your left first, which identifies all the main towns and hills visible from here. Continue to Rodney's Pillar, from where there are excellent views all around you.

From the pillar pass by the triangulation point to drop down, and then turn right on to a small, signed, grass footpath. This cuts through an embankment before dropping down through a stone wall to return you to the wide grass path junction, seen earlier. Do not cross the stile, but this time, turn left to follow this footpath downhill. Cross over a stile and continue to drop, as the path becomes rocky in places, descending steeply, and occasionally sharing the route with any excess rainfall.

Soon the path bears right, to follow the contour of the hill away from the cutting. This continues to drop and then bears around to the right before reaching another junction. Cross straight over on to the bridleway used earlier and drop back down to the wide forest track. Turn left and follow the permissive route once more to return to the car park.

POINTS OF INTEREST

■ *Admiral Lord George Rodney also fought during the American War of Independence, when the Royal Navy succeeded in capturing or destroying 21 American warships, 15 of these by Admiral Rodney.*

Looking across Shropshire

- The pillar used to be topped by a gold-coloured ball, but this was destroyed in 1835 by a lightening strike.
- Until they were demolished in 2003 six huge transmitters used to hide in the Severn Valley between the Breidden Hills and Welshpool. They were built to transmit messages between the Admiralty and Royal Navy ships during the Second World War.

OTHER WALKS IN THE AREA

Breidden Hill is one of three hills in this small range between Shrewsbury and Welshpool. Middletown Hill is the site of a hill

fort, with several routes stretching up from Middletown on the A458. It has also been designated as an area of Open Access, which means that, subject to any restrictions, it is possible to wander off the footpaths here. The highest of the three is Moel y Golfa at 403m (1,322ft), and there is a good path running up to and along its summit and back round to Middletown.

Overleaf: cows grazing on the Stiperstones with the Wrekin in the distance

Mid-Borders

WALK 10 | The Wrekin

The Wrekin may be only 407m (1,335ft) high, but, with few other mounds in the immediate vicinity, its presence is always obvious. Although it ranks outside the top five highest hills in Shropshire, the views from the summit certainly make up for it. On a clear day it is possible to see up to 15 counties.

Claims that it is an extinct volcano are false, although its rock is volcanic. However, the folktale of how The Wrekin came into existence is much more interesting. It is said that a Welsh giant wanted to flood the town of Shrewsbury and scooped up a huge handful of soil to dump in the River Severn. On his journey he stopped a cobbler near Wellington to ask how far it was to Shrewsbury. The cobbler, in fear that the giant would drown all his Shrewsbury customers, showed him a sack of disintegrated shoes, telling the giant that he'd worn them all out on his journey from Shrewsbury to Wellington. Put off by the distance he still thought there was left to travel, the giant dumped his soil and went back home, thus creating The Wrekin.

This walk takes in the summit of that pile of soil, with its fine, extensive views, before exploring its quieter wooded sides. Such is the magnetic draw of this fine hill for tourists and locals, you'll rarely find it devoid of walkers.

Walk category: moderate | Length: about 6km (3¾ miles) | Map: Explorer Sheet 242, Telford, Ironbridge and The Wrekin | Parking and starting point: lay-by on lane from J7 of M54; grid ref: SJ 638 093; other parking nearby | Public transport: none | Toilets: none | Nearest tourist information: Telford or Ironbridge

Toposcope on the summit of The Wrekin

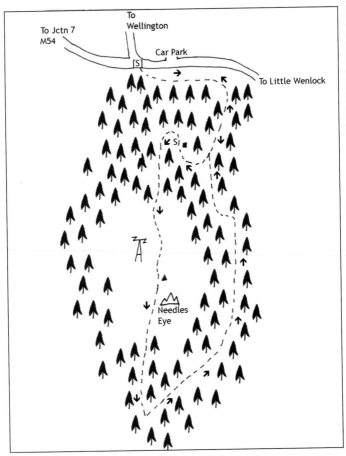

To Jctn 7
M54

To
Wellington

Car Park

[S]

To Little Wenlock

S

Needles
Eye

Map 10: The Wrekin

From the lay-by take the main track on your right, signed as a path but also stating that only authorised vehicles may enter. There is a transmitter at the top of The Wrekin and a dwelling halfway up, so take care because vehicles do use this track.

The Needle's Eye on The Wrekin

The Whalebacked Wrekin

The track passes some toilets (closed, unfortunately) on the right and begins to climb immediately. Follow it around to the right and ignore any smaller paths to the side. As it heads deeper into the trees, the track soon turns sharp right at a junction with a smaller path on the left and continues to climb, this time more steeply. The embankments on the side close in. By a dwelling on your right

take the small stile next to a double gate. Continue on the main track ahead, before it bends round sharply to the left. After a steady climb the track breaks out of the trees towards what looks like the summit – it's a false one, unfortunately – but after this, the track levels out for a short section before starting to climb once again. There are excellent views to your right and behind you.

The path levels out again and runs alongside a small copse of coniferous trees on your right. Continue to climb on the main track as it cuts between two small embankments to reach the final stage of the summit, which can clearly be seen from here, as can the transmitter. The toposcope at the summit details the main peaks and towns that can be seen from the 360-degree viewpoint.

After catching your breath, continue in the same direction, towards a rocky outcrop. Take time to bear left here to catch a glimpse of The Needle's Eye on the outcrop. Take extreme care because this area is unfenced. Returning to the path, follow it as it descends down in a southwesterly direction. Note that this well-defined track is much narrower than the route used to climb up because vehicles are not permitted on this section. The views from here extend over south Shropshire.

The path begins to drop more steeply between the trees, and at a crossing track turn left on to a path that climbs gently. This permissive footpath undulates its way through the lower wooded slopes of The Wrekin for some distance before reaching a junction with a footpath. Turn left on to this and follow it around the edge of the hill for about 1.5km (nearly 1 mile) until you reach a junction with a large track that you may recognise. Turn right and follow this downhill to return to the car park.

POINTS OF INTEREST

▮ *There are several folk tales relating to the Needle's Eye. Some say it was created by a giant's spade during a fight with his brother. Romantics say that a girl who meets a lad in the Needle's Eye will marry him. It is also said that a virgin who looks back when going through the eye will never marry. And when climbing through, always go west to east: it is bad luck going the other way around.*

▮ *The Wrekin is hundreds of millions of years older than Everest, the Alps or the Andes.*

■ *If you find yourself in a local pub, the Shropshire toast is 'All friends round The Wrekin'.*

OTHER WALKS IN THE AREA

The Ercall (pronounced 'arkle') is the smaller wooded hill between The Wrekin and Telford, reputedly created when the giant, who had already dumped the soil that formed The Wrekin, then stopped to clean the soil from the tread of his boots. There are several paths allowing you to explore The Wrekin forest. Nearby is Ironbridge Gorge, which although popular with tourists as a World Heritage Site, is perfect for following the Severn Way along the banks of the River Severn and the Shropshire Way footpath, which explores Benthall Edge Woods on the other side of the valley.

Welshpool is a delightful, bustling market town, and any visit has to be combined with a trip to nearby Powis Castle. It is only 4.8km (3 miles) from the border and has a very English feel about it. It is also an important gateway, and from here roads heading up the Severn Valley take travellers right into the heart of Wales, while the A458 is one of the main routes into the southern section of Snowdonia and towards the Welsh coast.

This walk takes you around the picturesque town, and there are plenty of opportunities to extend the walk by exploring Powis Castle, using the signed route from the town, or by doing some window-shopping. The walk also passes the Powysland Museum and Canal Centre. It then leaves Welshpool, following the towpath of the Montgomeryshire arm of the Shropshire Union Canal and allowing you to imagine what life was like when travelling was at a slower pace, before it returns to the car park at Buttington Cross.

Walk category: easy | Length: about 6.5km (4 miles) | Map: Explorer Sheet 216, Welshpool and Montgomery | Parking and starting point: British Waterways car park at Buttington Cross; grid ref: SJ 241 089; there are other car parks in Welshpool, where this route can be picked up | Public transport: Welshpool is on the Shrewsbury–Aberystwyth rail line; Arriva Midlands North service 75 (Shrewsbury–Llanidloes via Welshpool), Monday to Saturday (tel: 01543 466123) | Toilets: in Berriew Street car park, Welshpool, and Church Street car park, Welshpool | Nearest tourist information: Welshpool

---

Montgomery Canal near Welshpool

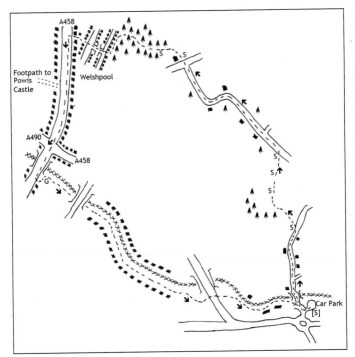

Map 11: Welshpool

From the British Waterway's car park and picnic site at Buttington Cross return to the lane and then turn right, crossing over the canal before continuing past some cottages on the left. Gently climb uphill. Where the lane forks, bear left and stay on this quiet lane as it winds its way uphill, with some good views of the Long Mountain behind you. Ignore any signed paths on the left and right and continue to climb, passing the occasional dwelling, until the tarmac lane eventually peters out and the route becomes a wide track.

Just before the track climbs more steeply, turn left to take a stile in the hedge into a field. Follow the left-hand boundary, but then cut through that boundary where there is a gap in the trees, to follow the same boundary, which is now on your right. Where the boundary turns sharp right, bear left towards the corner of the field and climb up to a stile. Cross this and continue ahead, allowing the field boundary on your left to bear away from you. Aim towards a stile to the left of a tree in the hedge in front of you. Before you reach this, however, there is another stile to cross in a wire fence, which soon comes into view. Cross over this and then climb up to the stile in the hedge.

Turn left to follow a tarmac lane with good views on your right. When you reach a triangular junction ignore the lane to the right and continue ahead. Ignore any signed paths on the left or right and follow this lane as it turns left and, shortly after, right before it begins to descend down to a junction with a road.

Cross straight over this road, then cross a stile on the right of a metal gate. Drop down on to a grass path between a hedge and a fence. Continue along here until the path forks, where you should bear left on to a wider track, through an embankment. Then drop down to a stile. Don't cross this, however. Instead, turn right downhill, bearing left on to a smaller track that has a stream on the right. Cross over a stile and follow this path into the trees.

As the route drops through the glade, it bears round to the left, before running along the backs of some properties, where it then drops down to a residential road. Continue down this road towards a mini roundabout at a junction, before turning right to drop down to reach the busier B4381, also known as Brook Street. Cross straight over this and continue along the passageway between two houses, emerging on to a lane and passing the Forestry Commission offices on your right. Cross straight over another lane to continue through another passageway to reach the main High Street in Welshpool.

Turn left and follow this downhill, passing plenty of opportunities for refreshments. Those interested in visiting Powis Castle should look for the signed route on the right next to Park Lane House, also on the right.

Country lane near Welshpool

To continue this walk follow the High Street, passing the town hall on your left, and continue down to the main crossroads. Go straight over, into Severn Street, passing the Royal Oak Hotel on your left. Soon you'll see the Powysland Museum and Canal Centre on your right, which is also worth a visit.

Continue over the canal, and then turn left into a picnic area with an information board about Glyndwr's Way. Leave this

picnic area by way of the gate by the canal and turn right to pick up the towpath. Follow this, under the Lledan Brook aqueduct, on its level route alongside the canal, continuing under a bridge and soon leaving Welshpool town centre behind. Near the outskirts, the canal bears left away from the towpath. Where this happens, take the towpath up to a junction with a road, turn left and cross the road at the zebra crossing. Turn right and continue over a side road, to take some concrete steps ahead, which drop back down on to the towpath.

Amble along the towpath, also signed as the Severn Way, under bridge 116 to leave Welshpool behind, passing fields on the other side of the canal. Just before you reach bridge 115, bear right up the steps and cross over the lane to return to the car park.

POINTS OF INTEREST

▪ *Welshpool was originally known as Pool, but was renamed in 1835 to distinguish it from Poole in Dorset on England's south coast.*
▪ *A Norman fort once stood where Powis Castle now stands, overlooking the Severn Valley. Its transformation into the palace seen today began in 1587.*
▪ *The Royal Oak Hotel acquired the 'Royal' only when Queen Victoria visited Powis Castle in the 19th century.*

OTHER WALKS IN THE AREA

Welshpool is the start (or finish depending on which way round you walk it) of Glyndwr's Way, which covers 212.4km (132 miles) via Machynlleth to Knighton. For a linear walk catch the bus from Welshpool to Berriew and follow the canal back. The tourist information centre can also provide details of other short walks around the town.

WALK 12 | Stiperstones

The Stiperstones are designated as a national nature reserve, and keen-eyed walkers may catch a glimpse of red grouse, while on a sunny day everyone will hear the musical song of the skylark. What makes this ridge different from the other hills in Shropshire are the quartzite outcrops that jut forcefully into the air. Created during the freezing process of the last Ice Age, which shattered the very hard rock, it has produced a landscape that has drawn people to it for thousands of years.

From this crest there are spectacular views across to Wales and glimpses of Shrewsbury to the north. Some of this short walk uses tracks on Open Access land, and you should, therefore, check for restrictions before tackling it.

Walk category: easy | Length: about 5km (3 miles) | Map: Explorer Sheet 217, the Long Mynd and Wenlock Edge | Parking and starting point: Stiperstones national nature reserve car park; grid ref: SO 370 977 | Public transport: Shropshire Hills shuttle bus, summer weekends only (www.shropshirehillsshuttles.co.uk) | Toilets: none | Nearest tourist information: Church Stretton

From the car park go through the small wooden gate, not far from the information panel, and climb up a wide, grassy track towards the rocky ridge. It's a relatively gentle climb. Ignore any tracks to your left or right as you wander up, remaining on the widest path. This soon begins to bear right gently, passing Cranberry Rock a little off to your left.

As you near the summit of the ridge, you reach a junction with a path that runs along the top. Turn right to follow this path along

The Devil's Chair

the ridge. Take care because it can be rocky in places and isn't particularly easy to walk along at a fast pace. The path soon reaches the next rocky outcrop on your left, Manstone Rock, which also has a triangulation point on its summit and is the highest point along this ridge.

Stay on the main path as it negotiates its way across the stony ground to the next outcrop, the Devil's Chair. The path cuts between this and another smaller outcrop on the right before

continuing in a downward direction. The views from here are excellent, with 180-degree panoramas stretching from mid-Wales, round to north Shropshire, The Wrekin, the Long Mynd and, in the distance, Brown Clee Hill.

Continue to drop down until you reach a wide crossing track. Turn right on to it and follow it round as it bears left, before dropping down to another path opposite a wooden gate. Don't go through the gate, but instead turn sharp right and follow this

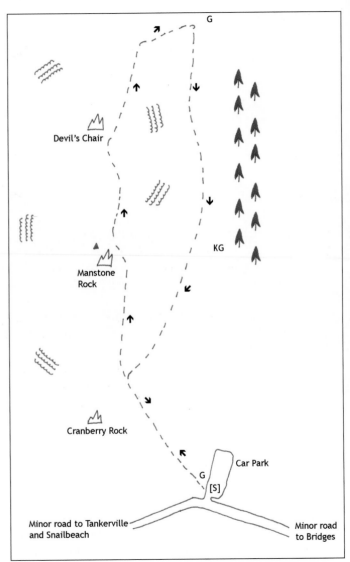

Map 12: Stiperstones

track, which runs roughly parallel with the stone wall and fence on your left.

Follow the track, which becomes rocky in places, as it begins to climb gently. Once it levels out it's a great vantage point to overlook the western edge of the Long Mynd on your left. Ignore a wooden kissing gate on the left and continue to follow this track. Stay on it where the fence turns sharp left downhill and continue until you reach the wide, grassy track you used to climb up to the top of the ridge. Turn left to drop back down to the car park.

POINTS OF INTEREST

- *Manstone Rock is the second highest point in Shropshire.*
- *Sour-tasting, bright red cowberries grow around here, but locally they are often called cranberries, which may explain why one of the quartzite tors is called Cranberry Rock.*
- *The Devil's Chair is reputed to have been created when the Devil, en route across Britain from Ireland, stopped for a rest on the highest outcrop on the Stiperstones. At the time, he was carrying stones in his apron to fill nearby Hell's Gutter. When he got up from his rest, his apron strings broke, sending the stones tumbling into a huge pile. Whenever he happened to be passing, he would sit down on this new rocky outcrop.*

OTHER WALKS IN THE AREA

Nearby is a visitor centre housed in an old school house, one of the few remaining buildings of the village called The Bog. Most of the village was demolished in 1972. Circular walks negotiate the former lead-mining region, and the Shropshire Way passes through. This area is much quieter than the more tourist-accessible Long Mynd.

Montgomery

Montgomery is a tiny town and has a very English feel about it, but that's understandable when you realise that it is about a kilometre (⅔ mile) from the border at its closest point. There is a dramatically perched, ruined castle on the cliffs overlooking the Severn Valley. Begun by Henry III in 1233, it replaced two earlier earthworks to the west of the town and was used to guard the Severn Valley trade route into mid-Wales. Standing at the edge of the castle, overlooking the cliff, the fertile fields below were the scene of a battle in 1644 when over 7,000 men fought for an hour in one of the bloodiest encounters of the English Civil War.

The contrast with today is astounding. Buzzards soar overhead, rape fields blossom in late spring, and bluebells carpet the wooded valley to the west of the castle. High on the summit of Town Hill is the Montgomeryshire war memorial, with an incredible view over the Vale of Kerry, mid-Wales and north Shropshire. Worthy of the climb, the walk allows you to admire these views, as well as to explore the castle and discover hidden country lanes.

Walk category: moderate | Length: about 9km (5½ miles) | Map: Explorer Sheet 216, Welshpool and Montgomery | Parking and starting point: at car park and picnic site on southern outskirts of Montgomery on B4385; grid ref: SO 224 963 | Public transport: Worthern Travel service 558 (Montgomery–Shrewsbury), (tel: 01743 792622) | Toilets: behind town hall, Montgomery | Nearest tourist information: Welshpool

View across the Severn valley from Montgomery Castle

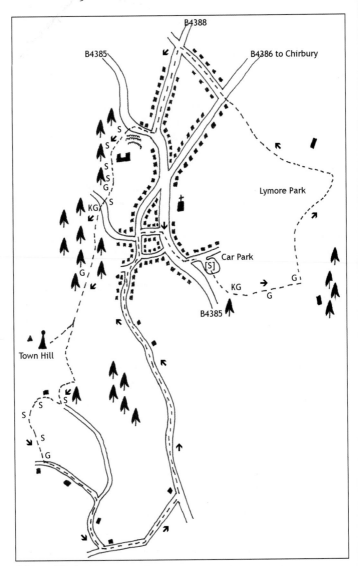

Map 13: Montgomery

Facing the playing fields, turn right to leave the car park, passing some picnic tables, to pick up a path through to Whitegate Pool picnic and wildlife area. Ignore the first bridge on the right but drop down to take the second bridge. Turn left to go through a kissing gate and then head across the field, keeping the hedge boundary on your left. You will soon pick up a track. Follow this to a gate into the next field. Go through it and continue along the track to reach a small gate on the left of a larger metal one. Pass through this and then turn left, as signed, on to a bridleway, which follows a tarmac drive through Lymore Park.

Continue over the cattle grid and follow this driveway as it arcs right, passing a lake on the right, before bearing sharp left. Ignore the signed footpath on the right and continue along the lane. There are good views from here of the castle ruins. Continue over another cattle grid, meander between two hedges and then bear right to climb up to the B4386.

Cross straight over this with care and continue on the quiet New Road, which has dwellings on both sides. At the junction with the B4388 turn left to return towards Montgomery, taking care of any passing traffic. Just after the veterinary centre on your left, pick up the tarmac pedestrian path and continue along here towards the Cottage Inn. Turn right, just before the junction with the B4385, to take some stone steps up to another tarmac pedestrian path on this B road. Turn right and follow this out of Montgomery.

Once you have passed the last house on the right, cross the road carefully and take the signed footpath on the left. Climb over the stile and bear diagonally right across the field to another stile in a fence. Cross this and then begin to climb through the wooded hillside on a small path that meanders between the trees. Soon the path bears right into a clearing, then turns left as it goes uphill, before reaching a stile on your right. Cross over this and turn left to follow the left-hand field boundary as you continue to climb uphill. Climb over the next

Broad Street, Montgomery

stile and continue along the left boundary, where you will catch
further glimpses of the castle.

Go through a large wooden gate and carry on up the track to
a stile. Cross this to reach a lane and then turn left, downhill.
Where the road bends to the right the entrance to the castle can
be found on your left. It is worth the diversion to explore the
castle ruins and the views over this pretty town.

To continue the walk, turn right and go through a metal kissing
gate, on to a path signed to the war memorial. This continues to
climb, bearing left before it reaches an embankment. Turn left to
follow the path until it joins a wide track. Follow this, climbing
steadily into a clearing. Soon the track bears left to a large

wooden gate. Go through the gate and continue on the wide track, which then begins to level out. The views across Shropshire open out on your left as the track continues along the ridge, passing the occasional coniferous tree before entering a new field.

Bear right, as signed, to climb up to the Montgomeryshire war memorial on the summit of Town Hill. The views extend across the Vale of Kerry and the Severn Valley as well as into parts of Shropshire. This is the only right of way to the war memorial, so to continue the walk return down the same path to the field corner once again.

Turn sharp right along the wide track with the field boundary on your left and the war memorial on your right. There may be livestock in this field. The path follows the left-hand field edge and carries through into the next field. Follow the path as it passes between the gorse bushes into a third field, keeping close to the left-hand boundary. Where a wide track crosses into the field on the left, follow into that field but continue downhill, with the boundary now close to your right. Follow this sharp right, as signed, before gently bearing left to a stile in the hedge ahead. Cross this and turn right on to a track.

Take this track past the entrance to Castell Y Gwynt and ignore the path on the right to stay on the track as it bears left. Before you reach the main gate for the dwelling, turn left over a stile to enter a field, and then turn sharp right. Follow this field boundary to the next stile, cross it and bear right to follow the field edge. Where this veers sharp right, bear left, as signed, down a small hollow, to a stile in a fence. Cross this and drop down through some trees with a fence on your right. Ignoring any side tracks, continue down to reach a small clearing, where the path follows the hedge on the left, until you see a metal gate on your right. Go through this to reach a small lane.

Turn left and climb uphill, between steep-sided banks, passing some dwellings on your right, where the lane soon levels. This quiet country lane then drops downhill before climbing once again to reach a junction with a telephone box on the right. Turn left on to this wider lane as it drops downhill to reach another junction. Turn left and follow this lane, which climbs gently. Take care along here. It is only a minor road, but locals use it frequently. Ignore a signed footpath on the right and follow this lane as it returns towards Montgomery. Soon the church and castle ruins come into view, and you pass a wooden bench on the left verge.

This lane then descends, passing some speed restriction signs and some residential roads on the right. Remain on this road until you reach a T-junction. Turn right and follow this road downhill. It then bears left. Ignore the road on your right and continue ahead to reach the top of Broad Street; the town hall will be in front of you (there are toilets behind here), and the Dragon Hotel on your left (good food). Turn right, down Broad Street, browsing through the shops, to reach the junction with Bishop's Castle Street. Turn right here and follow the road downhill, bearing round to the left and passing a children's play area on the left. Take the next road on the left to return to the car park.

POINTS OF INTEREST

- *When one of the pools in nearby Lymore Park was drained in the mid-19th century a helmet was found with the head still inside. It was thought to be a remnant from the Battle of Montgomery in 1644.*
- *Montgomery was granted a charter in 1227, allowing it to hold markets and fairs.*
- *Montgomery was named after the Norman lord, Roger de Montgomery, who was given the area by William I after the Conquest in 1066.*

OTHER WALKS IN THE AREA

There is a network of bridleways and footpaths through Lymore Park, making it possible to create a circular walk to Chirbury in England. Offa's Dyke path also bisects the park.

WALK 14 | The Long Mynd

The Long Mynd is a large, heather-clad plateau to the west of Church Stretton. There are several valleys, known locally as batches or hollows, the best known of which is Carding Mill Valley, owned, like a large swathe of the Long Mynd, by the National Trust, and this is where much of the car parking and the Trust's tea rooms and shop lie. Because of this, Carding Mill Valley is the tourist honeypot of the Long Mynd, and day-trippers from the Midlands often head out to this tight but idyllic valley.

Those visitors who climb out of the valley are in for a treat. Up on the top there are fewer people, although some do brave the single-track (but two-way traffic) road called The Burway, which in summer glimmers with the sheet metal of cars desperately trying to pass each other without dropping down the steep valley side. It is best to climb up on foot, however, to hear the skylarks singing as they climb into the air, and watch gliders soaring in the air.

This walk leaves Church Stretton by way of one of the quieter valleys, Townbrook Hollow, and climbs to the summit before dropping back down into Carding Mill Valley, giving you the opportunity to stop off at the National Trust café for a well-earned drink and a bite to eat. In winter the log fire there makes it even more enticing.

Walk category: moderate | Length: about 10.5km (6½ miles) | Map: Explorer Sheet 217, the Long Mynd and Wenlock Edge | Parking and starting point: Easthope Road car park by supermarket; grid ref: SO 454 936 | Public transport: Church Stretton is on the main Manchester–Cardiff rail line; Whittle Buses service 435

The Stretton Hills from the Long Mynd

(Shrewsbury–Ludlow via Church Stretton), Monday to Saturday (tel: 01584 872491) | Toilets: at Easthope Road car park, Church Stretton, and next to National Trust café in Carding Mill Valley | Nearest tourist information: Church Stretton

This walk begins from Church Stretton's main car park, which is in Easthope Road. If you are arriving by train, take the exit from the station signed to the town centre and follow this road round to the main road. Walk up the main road, passing a letter box and a convenience store on your left. Take the next left into Easthope Road and follow this to the car park on your right, just past the public toilets.

From the car park head towards the Bucks Head public house by a mini roundabout and turn right. Turn left by the market square up a quieter lane with the church on your left. Cross over the road and continue ahead between two stone pillars and then through a kissing gate into Rectory Woods and field. Follow the main path, which continues up some wooden steps. Take the kissing gate on your right and then turn right to follow a path that gently bears round to the left into the woods. Soon the sound of running water is audible, and a stream will become visible on your right. The path then turns right over a wooden bridge before bearing left around the edge of a small pond. Continue to follow the stream that is now on your left, climbing up to a kissing gate. Go through it and climb up to reach a junction of paths.

Cross over the main track to continue ahead, signed as Town-brook Hollow, with a metal fence and small reservoir on your left. You are now entering Townbrook Hollow, which is much quieter than its neighbouring Carding Mill Valley. The path continues to follow the stream as it gently meanders along the valley floor, but it soon begins to climb, leaving the stream behind. As it gets steeper,

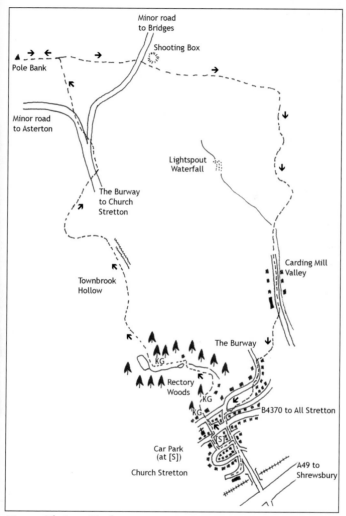

Map 14: The Long Mynd

Carding Mill Valley

stop to look back at the views of the hills on the other side of Church Stretton.

The path eventually bears around to the left at the head of the valley, crossing the beginnings of the stream once more. Look out for a wooden marker post on the right, and when you reach it veer to the right on to a grass path. Ahead you will see another wooden post. Follow the path around to the right to another

marker post where you join a larger track that is also a public footpath. Continue to climb. The path seems to disappear on the ground, but if you bear left, gently away from another market post, you'll soon notice the track on the ground again.

At the next marker post the path forks. Bear right and follow this path until you reach a tarmac road. This is the single-track The Burway, which climbs up and over the Long Mynd. It is popular with car drivers in summer and warm weekends, so take care. Cross over the lane and then turn left on the grass to walk alongside the road. Continue over a car parking area and on to a path alongside the road. Where the lane forks, leave the grass path and join the lane, bearing left, signed to the Midlands Gliding Club.

Soon the lane bears sharp left, and where it does so, continue straight ahead on to a wide bridleway. Climb uphill and at a large crossing track, turn left, continuing to climb. Within minutes, however, you will reach Pole Bank, the summit of the Long Mynd with a triangulation point and a toposcope, identifying the key hills that can be seen from the 360-degree view. On a good day, Cadair Idris near the Welsh coast can be seen, as can the Malvern Hills near Worcester.

Return along the same path, and when you reach the crossing track once more, continue straight over. Follow this until you reach a tarmac lane. Cross over this, passing a car park and then a shooting box on your left. Stay on this wide track along the top of the Long Mynd until you reach a large stone track. Bear left on to this for a short distance and then, where signed, turn right on to a wide bridleway leading to Carding Mill Valley.

Where the track forks bear right once more. It soon begins the descent into the valley, getting steeper as it falls. When you reach a path and stream joining from the right, cross over the stream and bear left to continue following the water downhill. Soon the path reaches a car park. Cross over a wooden bridge to follow the road, which can be busy in the summer and at weekends. This road fords the stream once more before passing the toilets and the National Trust café and shop on your right.

Shortly after this, bear right on to a signed bridleway that climbs out of the valley. Passing a house on your left, the track meets a road. This is The Burway once again. Turn left and follow, with care, downhill. On your left is a property called Kirklands and after this, on your left, is a small path. Take this and follow it round to the right by some railings to the town's war memorial. Pass by this and drop down to a small road. Turn left at the junction and continue to some crossroads. Take care and cross over and follow the main road, Sandford Avenue, with the town's shops downhill. Those parked in the car park should take the next road on the right, Easthope Road, to return to the car park. Rail passengers should continue ahead, bearing right where the railway station is signed.

POINTS OF INTEREST

- *Mynd is a corruption of the Welsh word* Mynydd, *which means mountain.*
- *The Midland Gliding Club, which operates from on top of the Mynd, is one of the oldest gliding clubs in Britain.*
- *Carding Mill Valley has appeared on a postage stamp.*

OTHER WALKS IN THE AREA

Ashes Hollow is another spectacular valley that can be accessed from Little Stretton to the south. On the other side of the valley there is access to Ragleth Hill and the impressive Caer Caradoc with its Iron Age hill fort. For something a little different, a wander around Helmeth Hill, the only completely wooded hill in the area, is spectacular in spring when the woodland floor is a riot of bluebells.

WALK 15 | Wenlock Edge

Wenlock Edge is an escarpment that runs for 24km (15 miles) from Craven Arms to Much Wenlock. Its western-facing edge is steep and forested for much of its length, but the eastern edge is much gentler. The B4371, Church Stretton–Much Wenlock road, follows the ridge for several kilometres, providing brief glimpses between the trees of the views on both sides.

Much of the area has been quarried and continues to be so today, although the National Trust has now acquired a large section of the Edge. This walk begins from one of the Trust's car parks and provides a walk of contrasts. There are times when the path wanders quietly through the trees with views across to the Stretton Hills in the west and The Wrekin in the north, yet it also follows the quarry edge with its hard landscaping but gentler views to the east.

Walk category: easy | Length: about 6km (3¾ miles) | Map: Explorer Sheet 217, the Long Mynd and Wenlock Edge | Parking and starting point: National Trust car park at Presthope on B4371; grid ref: SO 583 976 | Public transport: Whittle Buses limited service 860, Monday to Saturday, links Craven Arms and Much Wenlock (tel: 01584 872491) | Toilets: none | Nearest tourist information: Much Wenlock

From the car park take the main path towards the top of the Edge, where all the National Trust waymarked routes begin, and follow this round to the right and into the trees. Where this forks ignore the turning to the right and continue directly ahead, signed for

The Wrekin, as seen from Wenlock Edge

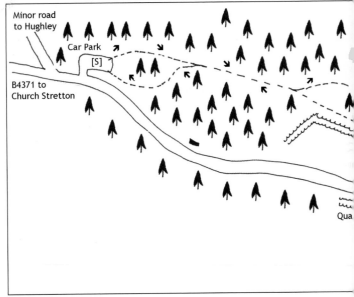

Map 15: Wenlock Edge

Knowle Quarry. Drop down some steps and continue briefly to climb up and then down some more steps, before reaching another set of steps to climb. Stay on this path as it meanders through the trees, which appear to skirt around the top edge of an overgrown quarry on your right, until you reach a junction.

Here, turn left to join what becomes a permissive path along-side the quarry. Take care along this section, because the fence between the path and the quarry is not the sort to prevent inquis-itive young children or dogs from straying over the edge. Follow this path for a distance, ignoring the signed turning on your left opposite some quarry buildings, where the Shropshire Way joins this path, and continue walking ahead. Keep watch for a view-point on your left in the trees offering great views over Shropshire.

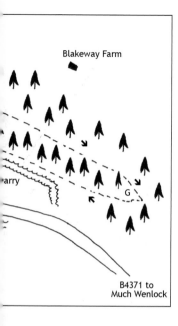

Blakeway Farm

arry

G

B4371 to
Much Wenlock

Where this track forks, bear left and drop steeply downhill to another wide track. Turn right and follow this through Blakeway Coppice. The National Trust is reviving the coppicing that once went on here and has even started making its own charcoal. Look out for the large, circular, metal containers that may or may not be smouldering. Follow this wide track. Where it splits, bear right to climb gently. This track soon levels out and continues through the coppice. Ignore a track on your right and stay on the main track, which is signed for Much Wenlock. Shortly after, there is a signed track on the left, which again should be ignored. Follow the main track as it climbs once more, rising to a large wooden gate. Go around to the right of the gate and before you reach a junction with another wide track, turn right on to a smaller path sandwiched between a fenced field and the trees.

Follow this smaller path as it regains the top of the Edge, with good views towards Brown Clee Hill. Soon the path rejoins the boundary with the large quarry here. Keep a watch on the right for a signed viewpoint called Major's Leap. A short diversion into the trees reveals a sudden drop, but there are extensive views over north and west Shropshire.

Continue along this main path alongside the quarry, ignoring a path on the right. Further along there is another viewpoint on your right, where the trees frame the iconic shape of The Wrekin in the

The view from Major's Leap

distance. This path soon reaches a junction with a track from the right, which you may recognise. Ignore this and continue ahead, to the end of the quarry where the path re-enters the trees.

At the junction of paths, ignore the track you came along from the car park, and this time bear left, signed to the Lime Kilns. Follow this through the trees, where the path soon drops down to a large track, above some kilns. If you want to explore these, turn left and follow the track down to the base of the kilns, where there is an interpretation board.

To return to the car park turn right above the kilns and follow the small path through the trees to pass Knowle Quarry on your

right, climbing up some steps to continue through the trees. At a junction with another path turn left, as signed, to return to the car park.

POINTS OF INTEREST

- *The National Trust owns about 13km (8 miles) of Wenlock Edge and manages the wood by coppicing and using the wood to produce charcoal by traditional methods.*
- *Wenlock Edge is actually the remains of a coral reef formed 400 million years ago.*

■ *Quarrying began when local people needed suitable building materials for dwellings. Today's larger quarries extract the rock for use in road construction.*

OTHER WALKS IN THE AREA

Use the Jack Mytton Way to walk in the other direction along Wenlock Edge to the National Trust's Wilderhope Manor and return via the Shropshire Way, through Easthope. There are several other waymarked walks from the National Trust car park here and at another car park on the B4371, on the outskirts of Much Wenlock.

WALK 16 | Brown Clee Hill

Brown Clee Hill is confusing. It is, in fact, two hills, called Abdon Burf and Clee Burf, yet despite being the highest point in Shropshire, neighbouring Titterstone Clee Hill appears taller and the Long Mynd attracts much more attention. Not only is Brown Clee Hill the highest point in Shropshire, at 545m (1,790ft), it's also one of the highest points in England south of the Pennines. Only Black Hill in Herefordshire, on the edge of the Brecon Beacons National Park, is higher. Brown Clee Hill offers some interesting views. To the west lie the Long Mynd, the Stiperstones and, on a clear day, Cadair Idris. To the north The Wrekin looks ominously isolated, while to the south is Titterstone Clee Hill, and to the southeast of that the rounded Malvern Hills.

Height always seems to tempt us to look towards the other hills and mountains, but look east from here and there is a very different view. It might come as a shock, but the Midlands are not flat. You cannot see Birmingham because of Kinver Edge in Staffordshire and the Clent Hills just south of Halesowen. On a clear day, however, you can make out the tower blocks in the direction of Wolverhampton.

Not only is there a contrast of views between east and west, but there is a contrast of countryside to be enjoyed during this walk. Brown Clee Hill is wild common and moorland, yet the second half of the route travels though the organised and neatly laid out Burwarton Park. Watch out for buzzards and sparrow hawks soaring above and listen for the recognisable rat-a-tat-tat of the woodpecker.

Walk category: moderate | Length: about 10km (6¼ miles) | Map: Explorer Sheet 217, the Long Mynd and Wenlock Edge | Parking and starting point: at side of country lane, opposite picnic site, northwest of Cleobury North; grid ref: SO 608 872 | Public transport: Whittle Buses service 141/142 (Bridgnorth–Ludlow), Monday to Saturday (tel: 01584 872491) | Toilets: none | Nearest tourist information: Bridgnorth

From the roadside parking continue up the lane briefly to take a signed path on the left. Go through a gate and then follow the path around to the right, before it bears to the left as it climbs. Shortly after passing a stone moneybox, the views begin to extend out to your left. Follow the path as it leaves the clearing and enters the woods with coniferous trees on the left and deciduous on the right.

Where the track forks, bear left to join a wide track in a clear drive through the woods. Shortly after turn right, as signed, through a small wooden gate and follow the wide path as it continues its journey uphill, before bearing around to the left. Eventually the path bears right once more to reach a wooden gate marking the boundary to Open Access land. Go through the gate and cross straight over the large crossing track, on to a smaller path through the trees. This soon leads into an area with fewer trees and the possibility of grazing livestock. Stay on this good path as it travels though this area, across a small stream and around to the left, and then rises to a steep section up an embankment.

At the top the route is relatively level for a short distance, with the remains of a stone crushing works unit on your right. Once again, the path rises steeply and at the top bears around the right-hand side of a small pool on your left before joining a tarmac track. Turn left on to this track and follow it round to the left, crossing a stile by a cattle grid. Continue on the tarmac driveway as it weaves its way around to the right, and just before you reach the transmitter turn left on to a wide track up to the summit, marked by the triangulation point. From here, you can see the Long Mynd, the

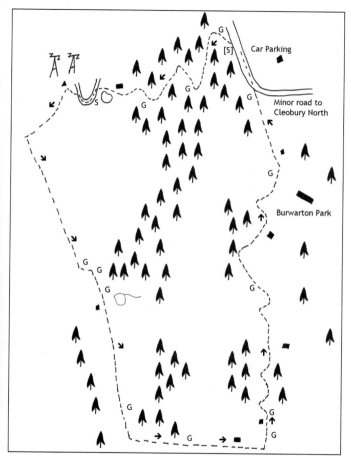

Map 16: Brown Clee Hill

Stiperstones, Corndon Hill, The Wrekin, Titterstone Clee Hill and the Malverns.

From the trig point and with the transmitter on your right, take the obvious path downhill on your left, which leads towards a fence line. When you reach the fence posts, turn left, as signed, on to a

View from Brown Clee overlooking Shropshire

wide track with a fence on your right-hand side. Follow this until the fence turns sharp right. From here, continue ahead in the same direction on a grassy path. This then drops down to a large metal gate at the top of a cleft between Abdon and Clee Burfs. Go through this and bear left towards a gate into the trees. After passing through this gate, ignore the next gate on your right, but take the smaller one that is beside the second large gate on your right.

Enter this field, which may have livestock in it, and follow the wide path around to the right, passing a stone ruin on your right, before climbing up to a gate. Go through and follow the main path, ignoring the path on the right and looking at the views on the left instead. This bridleway bears gently left, passing a pond on the left. Ignore a signed path on your left and continue through a wooden gate to remain on this bridleway. Cross straight

The trig point and view from Brown Clee Hill

over a wide track, with woods on the right and a field on the left, until you reach the end of this field. Turn left, as signed, on to a footpath that drops steeply, following the fence line on your left.

At a junction with a stone track continue in a downhill direction towards a metal gate. Go through and then bear right to stay on this bridleway as it continues to drop down. At a junction, turn left on to another signed bridleway, which soon passes a farm on the left. Take the gate next to the cattle grid and continue to

follow this wide bridleway (even though it is signed as a private drive). You are now entering the more formal parkland of Burwarton Park, which is used for animal grazing. Follow this as it meanders through the parkland, using the gate on the left of the next cattle grid, before zigzagging around the hillside. Continue straight over a waymarked path crossing from left to right, to remain on this bridleway as it bears round to the left to use a gate on the right-hand side of the third cattle grid.

Follow the bridleway around to the right, ignoring a large track that joins from the right, and then bear left, passing a cottage on the right. Ignore the next footpath on your left and bear right to reach a junction with a wide track. Bear left, as signed, to continue on the bridleway. Use the gate to the right of the fourth cattle grid and continue straight over the crossing track, ignoring another footpath that soon joins from the left. Shortly after, a footpath joins from the right, but the bridleway climbs gently, before descending down to the final cattle grid on the outskirts of the parkland. Use the gate on the left and turn left on to the quiet tarmac lane, following this gently uphill as it returns you to the car parking area.

POINTS OF INTEREST

▪ *Stone quarried from this area was used to pave many of the Midlands streets.*
▪ *The Burwarton Show, a one-day agricultural extravaganza that takes place at the beginning of August, dates back to 1891.*
▪ *During World War Two the highest hill in Shropshire claimed the lives of 23 airmen, whose planes, including a Lancaster Bomber and a Wellington Bomber, crashed into the hillside.*

OTHER WALKS IN THE AREA

The Shropshire Way continues up to the summit of Clee Burf, then down to Thorn Lane. Turn left here to pick up another bridleway to Nordy Bank Iron Age hill fort and then follow quiet country lanes to Abdon to pick up the Shropshire Way again, back up to the summit.

Bishop's Castle is exactly what it says it is. The original castle was built here by the bishops of Hereford, soon after the Norman Conquest in 1066, and records show that it existed in 1087. Keen to develop trade in the area, the Normans established a town here in 1127, and forty years later they built the stone castle, of which, unfortunately, little remains today. The Welsh name for this town was Y Trefysgob, which translates as 'the town of the bishops'.

Today, Bishop's Castle is a thriving rural town, with plenty of rolling hills to explore. This walk starts from the town centre and follows the Shropshire Way into the surrounding hills before coming back using an old droving road, the Kerry Ridgeway (see Walk 18 for more information). From here, the remains of the Bishop's Motte (moat) can still be seen, before descending back into Bishop's Castle to visit the castle remains and to make a little diversion to the town's independent brewery, the Three Tuns, for a refreshing drink.

Walk category: invigorating | Length: about 11.5km (7¼ miles) | Map: Explorer Sheet 216, Welshpool and Montgomery | Parking and starting point: main car park in Bishop's Castle; grid ref: SO 324 887 | Public transport: Minsterley Motors service 553 links Bishop's Castle with Shrewsbury (tel: 01743 791208); Secret Hills shuttle bus, summer weekends only (www.shropshirehillsshuttles.co.uk) | Toilets: at car park | Nearest tourist information: Church Stretton

From the car park, which is next to the livestock market, return to the main road and turn right to follow this round into Church Street. Turn left and head down towards the church. Where the road turns left, turn right, and then soon after, turn left into

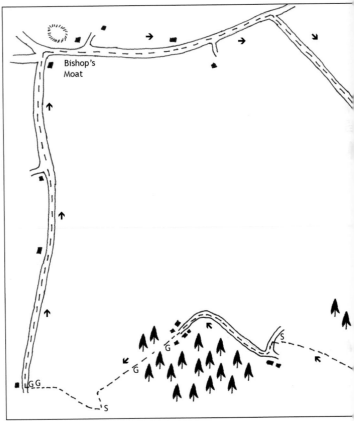

Map 17: Bishop's Castle

Church Lane. Follow Church Lane, past the fire station on your right, and take the next right, signed as Field Lane and waymarked as the Shropshire Way. Where this track forks, bear left, as signed, to continue along Field Lane.

Climb gently, eventually passing a few houses on your right. Continue through the gate to walk in front of a large house to reach a stile ahead, which is on the left of a large metal gate. Cross

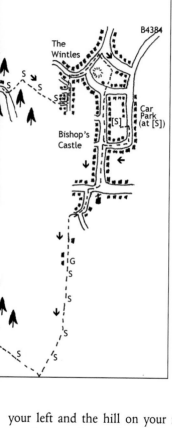

over this and continue on the Shropshire Way, which travels along a wide, grassy path. The views begin to open up on the left. Ignore a stile on the left and stay on this track to another stile on the right of a metal gate. Cross this and follow the track as it begins to descend. Soon the hedge on the right peters out, and the track descends to a stile on the left of a metal gate. Continue over this and follow the left-hand field edge.

Stay on this track into the next field. The waymark here suggests that you need to bear right, but keep to the left of the field to reach the next stile in the corner. Cross over and continue, but where the fence turns sharp left, go straight ahead, downhill, towards a stile and gate at the bottom. Do not cross these, but turn right, as signed, to wander through the field with the stream on your left and the hill on your right. Go over the stile beside a metal gate and cross the next field to another stile. All these fields may contain livestock, so beware. Cross this next stile and field to reach a stile at an angle to a metal gate. Climb over and proceed through another field, which may be boggy in places, until you reach a stile on the left of a metal gate. Cross over and drop down on to a tarmac lane.

Castle Street in Bishop's Castle

Turn left to climb up the hill gently and follow the lane round to the right. This meanders around the lower slopes of Colebatch Hill to reach the entrance to Middle Woodbatch farm. Ignore the stile on your right and continue ahead on the wide stone track. As you approach the farm buildings, fork to the right to continue climbing, and you will soon pass a confirmation waymark. Climb past these farm buildings, and just before this wide track forks take the small gate on your left on to a path that climbs up between the trees. This climbs steeply, with Henley Wood on your left but soon with views opening out on your right. Climb up to a small metal gate and continue ahead, as waymarked.

Follow the fence line, as signed, to the right but look out for the waymark on that fence, pointing you left and uphill. Turn here and climb up to a stile on the right of a metal gate. If you look back, you'll see some good views of Bishop's Castle, the Stiperstones and the Long Mynd. Cross over the stile and turn right to follow the fence, all the way around to a large metal gate. Proceed through this, passing a farm building on your left to remain on this track to another gate. Go through this to reach a tarmac lane.

Turn right and follow this quiet, single-track lane as it gently drops downhill, with some good views on both sides. After passing some buildings on the left, the lane gently climbs. Where a lane joins from the left, continue ahead, signed to Bishop's Castle. At the next junction, turn right on to a wider lane, still signed to Bishop's Castle but also waymarked as the Kerry Ridgeway. Immediately to your left there are good views towards Montgomery, and then soon after, in a field on your left, you can see the remains of Bishop's Motte (moat) earthwork (private land).

Continue along this lane and ignore the lane on your left and the next one on your right for Woodbatch Farm. Turn off the Kerry Ridgeway to take the next lane on your right, which is signed to Lydbury North. Ignore any paths on both sides of the lane and follow this narrow lane downhill to pass some buildings on the left. Follow the lane round to the left, and then where it turns right, turn left on to a signed footpath. Cross over a stile and a wire fence to enter a field and drop downhill. Turn right to a stile in the hedge. Cross over this and bear left to the next stile in the hedge opposite.

Cross this and continue down towards the houses. Cross another stile to enter a residential road, Oak Meadow. Follow this to the junction and turn left, uphill, passing a small cul-de-sac on your left, and then passing numbers 80 and 82 on your right, to take a footpath with metal barriers up to join Welsh Street Gardens. Continue uphill to reach the next junction with Welsh Street, opposite an environmentally friendly housing estate, called The Wintles. Turn right and follow Welsh Street, taking Castle Street on your left. Climb up. To visit the castle remains use the stone steps on your right. Although there is little of the castle left today, this is a pleasant spot for a well-earned rest.

Return to Castle Street and turn right to follow it round. Take the narrow footpath on your right, between two properties,

Meadow near Bishop's Castle

signed to the town centre. This passes the bowling green on your right (which was once the centre of the castle) and then drops downhill, bearing left to descend into Bull Street. Turn right and drop down to reach crossroads. For those walkers who have worked up a thirst, turn left into Salop Street to visit the Three Tuns Inn and brewery, with its small museum on the history of brewing. Otherwise, cross straight over towards the Market Square, but then bear left, signed for Clun, into the High Street. Drop down past the town hall on your right and various shops on

both sides, to return to Church Street, turning left into Station Street to follow it back round to the car park.

POINTS OF INTEREST

- *Bishop's Castle has two home-brew inns: the Three Tuns, which dates from 1642, and the Six Bells Brewery Tap.*
- *The Bishop's Castle Railway ran from 1865 for 70 years, 69 of them in receivership.*

■ *The tower of the Church of St John the Baptist has a unique one-handed clock.*

OTHER WALKS IN THE AREA

As home to an annual walking festival, there are plenty of opportunities around here. Follow the Shropshire Way north to pass the motte and bailey embankments of Lydham and More or head east towards Oakley Wood.

WALK 18 | Kerry Ridgeway

The Kerry Ridgeway was a popular route for cattle and sheep drovers on their journeys from mid-Wales to the English markets some 150 years ago, although the origins of the route are said to predate the Iron Age. The views from here, at over 305m (1,000ft), stretch far across Wales and Shropshire. Sandwiched between the Severn Valley and the beginnings of the River Teme, this walk really does feel as if it's on top of the borders. The Kerry Ridgeway is a walk to be shared – it is a bridleway, so is popular with horse riders and cyclists – but it's a perfect vantage point to look down on soaring buzzards and the occasional red kite.

This circular walk follows the Ridgeway west towards Kerry Hill, then drops down into a quiet valley where a tributary of the River Teme babbles near your feet, before taking some quiet country lanes to climb back up to Nantyrhynnau Wood and pick up the Kerry Ridgeway once again.

Walk category: moderate | Length: about 11km (6¾ miles) | Map: Explorer Sheet 214, Llanidloes and Newtown | Parking and starting point: Forestry Commission car park and picnic site at Block Wood; grid ref: SO 149 863 | Public transport: Shropshire Hills shuttle bus, summer weekends only (www.shropshirehillsshuttles.co.uk) | Toilets: none | Nearest tourist information: Newtown

From the car park cross over the B4368 and go through a large metal gate to join a wide track. This follows a fence line on your right, with excellent views across the Severn Valley. Follow this track, ignoring the signed bridleway on the right. The track passes the edge of a wood on your right before climbing up

Map 18: Kerry Ridgeway

towards a metal gate. Go through the gate and continue, with the fence now on your left. The views on this section extend for some distance in both directions.

Continue past a transmitter on your left and go through another metal gate, then climb gently up to the next metal gate. Go through, and stay on the obvious track as it begins to level out. Ahead, you might be able to see the turbines of the large wind farms near

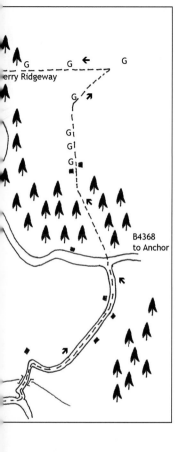

Llandinam. Continue ahead through another gate and follow the track as it bears around a small pool on the left, and then up to another gate. Go through this and follow the fence line on your right to reach a junction of waymarks.

Turn left on to a signed bridleway uphill, with the trees on your right and bear left to a metal gate in the fence. Pass through into a field and head across as waymarked to a gate on the other side. Go through this and cross the next field, bearing right to its corner beside a wood. Pass through a gate and climb uphill, bearing right to then drop down to another metal gate in the fence line. Go through, turn left as waymarked to another wooden marker post and then bear right on a small path with the stream on your right. At the next waymark post turn right on to a wider grass path and follow this downhill.

This meanders and eventually becomes a substantial track, crossing the stream to climb up to a series of gates. Pass through three gates in quick succession to enter a field as waymarked. Cross the field and then bear left on to a track that drops down to pass a stone farm building on your right. Continue around this building and go through a metal gate into the next field, bearing

right to join a wide track. Turn left to follow this near to the ridge, which drops sharply on your left to the stream. Bear left to take a wide track to the left of a line of trees, which soon disappears, and take care as you drop down the end of the ridge, bearing right through a gap in the line of trees to reach a metal gate on your left. Go through and bear right, crossing the stream and picking up a path on the other side, which gently climbs.

Where this small path forks, with an obvious grass path heading uphill, bear right to stay on the smaller path, and follow the bankside, high above the stream, to reach a waymark post. Continue ahead, as signed, to another waymark post to reach a wide track. Turn right here and follow this to cross over the stream again, this time using a wooden bridge. Follow the wide track ahead, through a metal gate, and alongside a line of trees on your left, over a crossing track, and then gently downhill. This track bears gently left before arriving at another metal gate.

Go through this and continue ahead on to a tarmac lane. Ignore the lane on the right and continue ahead, passing several farm buildings. The lane passes between wire fences on both sides, before bearing gently left and climbing. Eventually it levels out, before dropping down to reach a quiet junction. Turn left, signed to Anchor, on to a quiet lane, which drops downhill, crosses the stream again and then climbs. This lane meanders between fields, with the Cefn Vron Plantation visible at times on your right. After passing a farm, the lane begins to climb. Look out for the earthwork remains of Castle Bryn on your right at the end of the plantation.

Pass two houses on your right, Newcwm Farm on your left and then a pond on your right, cross over a stream and then climb up the lane to meet the junction with the B4368. Turn left here. Shortly after, turn right, on to a footpath signed to the Kerry Ridgeway. Follow this as it negotiates its way through the closely planted trees of Nantyrhynnau Wood, as waymarked, until you

The Kerry Ridgeway

Looking over the Vale of Kerry

reach a junction with some wide forest tracks. Cross straight over and continue on one of these wide tracks as it continues to climb. Ignore the signed bridleway on your left and continue ahead, as signed, over a cattle grid. Then bear left, around a farm building, on a track that climbs up to a metal gate. Go through and follow this wide track between two fences, passing through a couple of other gates to reach a plateau.

Follow the track, with the fence on your right, and continue under the telegraph wires to reach a gate on your right. Go through and cut diagonally right across this field towards a waymark beside a wooden gate. At this junction of paths, don't cross into the next field but instead turn left to rejoin the Kerry Ridgeway, where there are some splendid views again across the

Severn Valley. Go through a gate and enter the next field, to pick up a substantial track that runs alongside a wood on your right. At the end of this field, go through the large wooden gate on to a wide forest track and follow this downhill to return to the car park.

POINTS OF INTEREST

- *The Kerry Ridgeway bridleway begins near Cider House Farm on the B4355 and stretches for 24km (15 miles) to reach Bishop's Castle.*
- *The Ridgeway never drops below 305m (1,000ft) above sea level.*
- *Views to the west extend as far as Plynlimon, which is the source of the River Severn.*

OTHER WALKS IN THE AREA

A different circular walk uses the Ridgeway to reach the Ceri Forest and then passes along quiet lanes to drop down into the village of Kerry, before using lanes to return to Kerry Hill. Glyndwr's Way passes nearby at Felindre, which can be used with other paths to reach Beguildy, before crossing the young River Teme and returning to Felindre.

It had to happen at some point, but this is the only walk in this book that uses two Ordnance Survey maps. It is worth it though. On a warm summer's day nothing can beat the quiet climb through the small lanes into the Forestry Commission woods of Steppleknoll and Sunnyhill, up to the summit of the Bury Ditches Iron Age hill fort, with views over A.E Housman's 'blue remembered hills'. From here the walk drops down into the Clun Valley and the sleepy village of Clunton, before crossing the River Clun to return through Sowdley Wood, where it skirts past the last home of the playwright John Osborne, author of *Look Back in Anger*. Dropping back down into Clun, the walk passes the church where Osborne and his wife are buried, before passing Clun's medieval stone arched bridge and the romantic remains of its stone castle.

The Clun Valley was popularised by the poet A.E Housman in his 1896 collection *A Shropshire Lad* with the lines:

Clunton and Clunbury,
Clungunford and Clun,
Are the quietest places
Under the sun.

Anyone who follows this walk will wholeheartedly agree.

Walk category: Invigorating | Length: about 14km (8¾ miles) | Maps: Explorer Sheet 201, Knighton and Presteigne, and Explorer Sheet 216, Montgomery and Welshpool | Parking and starting point: Clun community area car park; grid ref: SO 302 812 | Public transport: Shropshire Hills shuttle bus, summer weekends only (www.shropshirehillsshuttles.co.uk); Whittle Buses service 745, Monday to Friday (tel: 01584 872491) | Toilets: Clun Castle car park | Nearest tourist information: Church Stretton

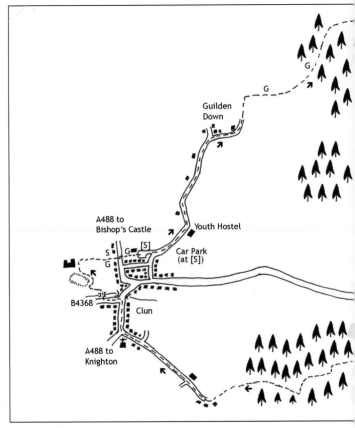

Map 19: Clun

From the Clun community area car park return to the road and then turn left to follow this quiet lane, soon passing the youth hostel on the right. Continue past a couple more dwellings, ignoring the Shropshire Way on your left, as the lane begins to climb gently. Ignore the stile on your right and, later, a bridleway on the right where the lane bears left and climbs more steeply. The Shropshire Way rejoins the lane on the left as it climbs, passing

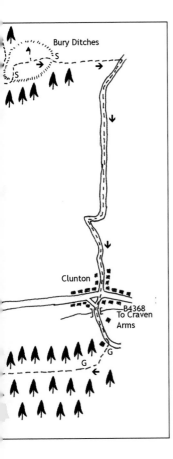

some further cottages on your left before it reaches a farm. Where the lane forks, bear right between the farm buildings, ignoring another signed path on the left.

This lane is level. Immediately after a cottage on the left turn left, as signed, on to a bridleway track that climbs uphill. After passing the entrance to a cottage on the right, followed by two field entrances on the left, you will reach a metal bar gate. Go around this and follow the tree-lined track all the way to another metal gate. Pass this and climb steeply, passing a small pond on the right. Continue over a crossing track, before bearing left to reach a junction with a wide forest track.

Turn right and follow this level section, ignoring the first track on your right. Soon the track drops slightly. You should ignore tracks on your right and left until you reach a fork. Bear left here, signed as the Shropshire Way, and climb. Ignore the tracks on your left and right to stay on this wide path, which remains signed as the Shropshire Way, until you reach the highest point of this path. At this point, beside a small wooden bench, turn right into the trees to follow a path also signed as the Shropshire Way along with other colour-coded Forestry Commission walks. Continue along this route as it bears

Clun Castle

left, eventually reaching a junction with a gate and stile into the Iron Age hill fort area of Bury Ditches, which will be on your left. Turn left to cross the stile and follow the wide, grassy path up between the ramparts into the centre of the earth mound. At a waymark post turn left to reach the summit with its informative toposcope and great views.

Return to the waymark by the same path and turn left to follow this wide, grassy path down through the other side of the ramparts to reach another stile and gate. Cross this and continue on the stone path that drops in a straight line, offering good views to your right. Where the path forks, bear left on to the grass route to reach a picnic site and car park, bearing left to reach the entrance at a lane.

Housman's Blue Remembered Hills of the Clun Valley

Turn right here and follow this lane as it first descends, then bears left and climbs to pass some farm buildings on the right. The views along this section, as the lane follows the contours of the hill, are beautiful. Soon the lane turns left and begins its long descent for a further 1.6km (1 mile) down into the village of Clunton, where a small brook follows the left-hand side of the road.

At the crossroads, take care and cross straight over the B4368, to follow a lane between the brook and the Crown Inn. The lane then bears left and crosses the River Clun. Ignore the lane on the immediate left and continue ahead, towards a cottage on your

right. After this cottage is a signed bridleway on the right. Go through the metal gate and climb steeply between the hedges into Sowdley Wood. Go through a wooden gate, as signed, to join a wider, more level track. Shortly afterwards a large forest track joins from the left. Ignore this and continue ahead, as signed, as it remains level through the trees. Glimpses of the Clun Valley can be seen on the right. Soon the track climbs gently before zigzagging its way around some clefts in the hillside. Continue to stay on this main wide track, ignoring the side paths. Soon the route bursts out of the trees between arable fields.

Where a track joins from the right, continue ahead. There are some excellent views over the village of Clun on your right. Continue ahead where a bridleway joins from the left and begin to drop down towards some cottages. At a junction with a tarmac lane, turn right, where the route climbs up to a small road junction at the summit. Continue ahead, signed to Clun, as the lane descends, passing a small memorial and seat on your left. Ignore a stile on your right to stay on the lane as it descends to cross a stone bridge over a small stream before climbing to another junction. Turn left here and follow this lane through the outskirts of Clun to reach the junction with the A488.

On the left is St George's Church, where John and Helen Osborne are buried. If you wish to visit the graves climb up through the lich-gate towards the main entrance, but before there turn right on to a small path. The graves are on the right.

From the church turn right, downhill, using the pedestrian path. Just before you reach the medieval bridge, turn left to pick up the B4368 again. It's a picturesque spot here by the river. Shortly after, turn right into the castle car park. Aim for the wooden footbridge that is to the right of the toilets. Cross over the bridge and turn right to climb some steps up to a wide path. Turn left and, at the junction with the lower ramparts of the castle, bear right to follow the trough between two embankments. Where this opens out continue ahead to climb up to a wide track beside the bowling green. Take time to explore the castle by turning left here. Once you've done that, return to this point and head towards the gate to exit the castle grounds. You can either use the stile on the right or the smaller gate on the left to continue ahead on a wide track to reach the main road.

Take care, because there are no pavements, and turn left for a short section, turning right through some metal railings on to a small footpath. Follow this beside a children's play area on the left and then around a gate to follow the main track alongside the community centre on your left to bring you back to the car park.

POINTS OF INTEREST

- *E.M. Forster called Clun Oniton in his 1910 novel* Howard's End.
- *Clun was also the setting for the children's book* The Secret of Grey Walls *by author Malcolm Saville.*
- *Sir Walter Scott once stayed here, and it is believed that the Castle of the Garde Doloureuse in his novel* The Betrothed *(1825) is based on Clun's fortress.*

OTHER WALKS IN THE AREA

Several forest trails around Bury Ditches are worth exploring, and anyone wanting to explore the upper reaches of the Clun Valley can do so by using the Shropshire Way to the village of Whitcott Keysett and then following a quiet lane to link up with Offa's Dyke, returning to Clun by way of the Jack Mytton Way.

Stokesay Castle is actually a fortified manor house, not a castle. It is, however, one of the earliest such manor houses in England – parts date from the 12th century, although the great hall was built in the 13th century – as well as one of the finest and best-preserved fortified manor houses in England. The timber-framed gatehouse and crenellated tower are perfectly poised for any postcard, yet they contrast perfectly with the grass-roofed, curved structure of the nearby Shropshire Hills Discovery Centre. One of Shropshire's millennium projects, the Discovery Centre sits in a 10 hectare (25 acre) site alongside the banks of the River Onny and provides plenty of other walking opportunities as well as a welcome café for the end of this walk.

The walk begins from the Discovery Centre and heads towards the castle, from where it leads into the Clun Valley, gently climbing to the top of the National Trust property, Hopesay Hill. Quiet country lanes take the route to Aston on Clun with its well-known Arbor Tree and then back round to Stoke Wood, giving you the opportunity to visit Stokesay Castle properly before returning to the Discovery Centre.

Walk category: invigorating | Length: about 15.5km (9½ miles) | Map: Explorer Sheet 217, the Long Mynd and Wenlock Edge | Parking and starting point: Shropshire Hills Discovery Centre, Craven Arms; grid ref: SO 435 825 | Public transport: Whittle Buses service 435 (Shrewsbury–Ludlow), Monday to Saturday (tel: 01584 872491); Craven Arms is on the Manchester–Cardiff rail line; Broome is on the Heart of Wales Railway Line | Toilets: at Shropshire Hills Discovery Centre | Nearest tourist information: Church Stretton or Ludlow

From the Shropshire Hills Discovery Centre car park take the path that leads around the left-hand side of the building, towards Onny Meadows. When you reach a junction ignore the path to the left and continue ahead. Where the path forks beside a stone maze, bear right. Ignore the path on the left and continue ahead over a small wooden bridge on to either of the grassy paths (it makes no difference). Both paths meet at a junction with a larger track. Bear right up to a metal gate. Go through the adjacent kissing gate and take extreme care when crossing the A49.

Once across the road, turn left on to a tarmac path and follow this between a hedge and a lay-by. At the junction with a lane, turn right and follow the lane past the Church of St John the Baptist and then around to the left. Continue past the castle and then turn right through a large metal gate on to a track that leads you around the right-hand side of a pond. There may be livestock here. Go through a metal gate, under the railway and then through another metal gate. Turn right into a field and head towards a metal gate in the hedge line. Bear to the left of this as waymarked, and follow the right-hand field edge. Cross over a stile beside a metal gate and continue along the next field boundary on your right. Ignore the stile and signpost in the boundary on your right and continue climbing gently. At the field corner bear right to cross a stile into the woods. Follow this path through the trees, ignoring a small track on the left, and drop down to pass over a stile on the right. The path drops straight down the field edge to the bottom. At the field corner turn left to continue around to a stile in the next corner. Cross this and turn right on to a lane. Go under the railway bridge and at a junction with the busy B4368, taking care as you cross, go straight over to continue ahead on to a small lane.

After a short distance turn left over a stile between some double metal gates next to a parish notice board. Follow this along the left-hand field boundary, crossing another stile beside a metal gate and then continuing to the next stile. Cross this to continue along

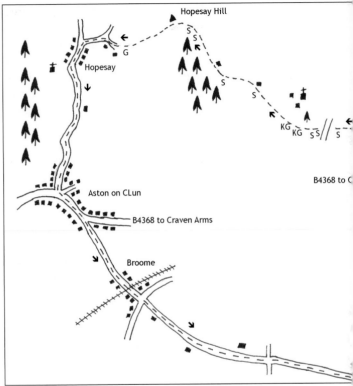

Map 20: Craven Arms

the left-hand field edge. Turn left, as signed, over a stile by a gate, but when you are in the field bear right to follow the right-hand field edge. After a short distance, bear left into the field towards a waymark post beside a small wooden bridge that crosses a ditch. Go over this bridge and head for the stile in the hedge. Cross this, cross straight over a lane and then climb up to cross two more stiles in quick succession to enter a field. Aim for the waymark ahead (to the left of a large tree at the brow of a hillock) and from there continue across this field as waymarked to reach a kissing gate.

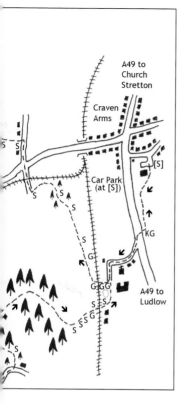

Go through this gate, cross over a driveway and go through another kissing gate to follow the path to a bridge with a stile at both ends. Cross this and then bear right, away from the telegraph poles, to another waymark ahead in the field, crossing a small ditch in the process. From this waymark continue ahead to find a stile to the left of a small cottage. Continue over this and climb up between the trees, and then bear slightly left at the tree line, as signed. Climb up the hill, bearing left, to reach a stile by a metal gate in the diagonally opposite field corner. Cross this and follow the track as it arcs its way uphill. Entering a field, keep to the left-hand field boundary alongside the wood, following this round to the right.

Turn left where signed to take a track uphill. This will take you past a derelict building on the right and up to a stile by a metal gate. Continue over this and maintain the left-hand field boundary. At the top of the hill, cross over another stile by a metal gate to enter Hopesay Common, which is National Trust property.

Continue ahead to drop downhill gently at first, ignoring the wider, more definitive, grass path to your left. There are good views from here. As you continue downhill, the path on the ground becomes more defined between the bracken and drops more steeply as it goes around to the left. At a junction with a wider track, turn

Stokesay Castle

left then immediately right to continue down through a wooden gate on a path hedged on both sides. At the junction with a lane, turn left, passing Brookside Cottage on your left. At the next lane junction turn left into the heart of Hopesay village. At the junction turn left and follow this road through the quiet village.

Ignore a lane on your right and continue to follow this road for just over 1.6km (1 mile) to reach the village of Aston on Clun.

Cross over the stream to reach the main B4368 once again, with the village's Arbor Tree on your left. Don't take Mill Street on your left. Instead, continue ahead on the pedestrian path through the village, passing the Kangaroo Inn on your right. A bit further round are the village stores and The Round House.

Take the road on the right, signed to Broome, and follow this the short distance to this village, passing the Engine and Tender

House pub on your left and, later, passing the entrance to Broome railway station on the right, just before you go under the railway line. At the crossroads with the busy B4367 take care to cross straight over on to a narrow lane. This quiet lane gently climbs, passing a couple of isolated properties. Just after Rowton Villa on your left, the view to the right over the Clun Valley is lovely.

At the next crossroads continue straight over and begin the ascent up towards the woods. The lane here becomes quite steep in places, but the views behind are worth stopping for. Just as you reach the top of the hill, turn sharp left, immediately before a house, to follow a path between two fences. When you reach a stile cross this and drop down into the trees. Follow the path, as signed, along a field edge briefly – again, there are excellent views over the Clun Valley – before re-entering the woods. At a field corner turn right on to a wider track. Follow this down through the trees and around to the right. When you enter a field keep to the right-hand boundary.

Cross over the stile and continue along the field boundary, turning left where signed, and drop down in front of a property. At a gravel track turn right to continue past the dwelling and take the stile beside the large tree. Turn right on to a wide forest track and follow this through the trees. Some felling has taken place, so this is not thick woodland. Continue along here to a junction that is waymarked. Turn left into the trees to reach a stile. Cross over this to enter a field, and then bear right towards the next stile in the hedge. Good views can be seen here of Stokesay Castle. Cross this and continue over the next field. Cross another stile and field to reach a large metal gate. Go through here to follow the farm track to the railway line.

Exercise extreme care when crossing the railway line. Use the stiles beside the gates on both sides. Once across, follow the farm track around the right-hand side of the pond. Go through the double metal gates to turn left on to a lane. Follow this and, if you have time, explore Stokesay Castle (English Heritage) on your

Shropshire Hills Discovery Centre

right. Follow the lane back towards the A49, but turn left to use the tarmac path alongside the lay-by once more. Take care as you turn right to cross the A49, and then re-enter Onny Meadows by using the kissing gate, turning left to return to the car park.

POINTS OF INTEREST

- *Stokesay Castle was involved in only one military encounter. During the English Civil War it surrendered, without any fighting taking place.*
- *Tree dressing, which is believed to date back to the Bronze and Iron Ages, is a ritual that was intend to promote fertility, both within the local community and of their land. Charles II introduced Oak Apple Day on 29 May (his birthday), when villages would dress trees as a sign of allegiance to him. In Aston on Clun the ceremony has survived due to the foresight of John Marston who set up a trust in 1786 to pay*

for the upkeep of the Arbor Tree and the flags. Tree dressing and extra activities still take place here on the last Sunday in May.

■ *Craven Arms is the only town in Shropshire created because of the railways. Lying at the junction of several valleys, with branch lines from mid-Wales and Much Wenlock connecting with the Shrewsbury–Hereford line, Craven Arms became a major trading point for sheep. The town grew to accommodate this trade, although, sadly, only the Shrewsbury–Hereford and the Heart of Wales lines still exist.*

OTHER WALKS IN THE AREA

The Shropshire Hills Discovery Centre has several waymarked routes that begin from its grounds, some of them using the old railways lines that are no longer in use. Routes vary in length from the gentle Riverside Ramble at 3.2km (2 miles) to the more vigorous 13.7km (8½ mile) Wart Hill Wander. For more information visit www.shropshire.gov.uk/discover.nsf.

The Heart of Wales Railway Line is one of the most scenic single-track routes in Wales. It leaves the main Manchester–Cardiff line at Craven Arms and cuts through the borders, crossing into Wales near Knighton. The first stop after Knighton is Knucklas, a quiet village nestling at the foot of the Radnorshire Hills and on the edge of the Teme Valley.

There is no designated car parking in Knucklas, so drivers are asked to park considerately where possible, but the best way to arrive in the village is by train. You'll need to advise the guard that this is where to you want to get off because many of the smaller stations on this walk are request stops only. For your return journey you'll need to stick out your arm, as if hailing a bus, to get the train to stop.

This walk follows quiet country lanes for its entirety, so there is no need to look out for stiles, waymarks or gates. There are a couple of steep sections, but you should be able to cope even if you have children in pushchairs. Watch the buzzards circling above and rabbits darting across fields, and marvel at the views over the isolated hills that can be seen from the highest point on the walk.

Walk category: easy | Length: about 8km (5 miles) | Map: Explorer Sheet 201, Knighton and Presteigne | Parking and starting point: no designated car park (park in the village); grid ref: SO 254 741 | Public transport: Knucklas is served by the Heart of Wales Railway Line; Sargeant Brothers East Radnor Circular (Knighton–Knucklas–Lloyney) bus service (tel: 01544 230481) | Toilets: none | Nearest tourist information: Knighton

---

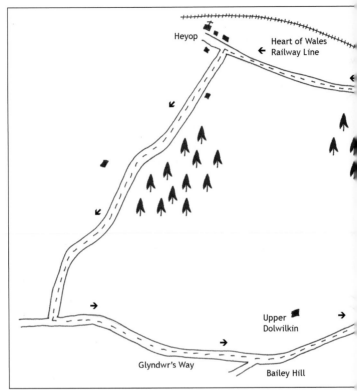

Map 21: Knucklas

From the railway station drop down into the residential road and follow it downhill to a junction. Turn left, passing a bus stop, and head towards Castle Inn. Where the road forks, bear right and drop gently downhill so that there are properties on your left and a stream on your right. Where the road forks, bear left, away from the stone bridge, along a lane signed to Heyop. Ignore the lane on your left and continue underneath the viaduct as it cuts across the valley, ignoring another lane on your left on the other side of the viaduct. Soon you pass Heyop Road on your right, and the lane leaves

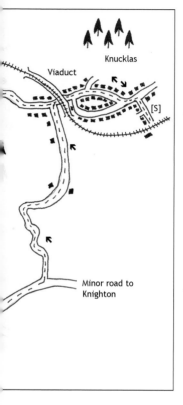

Knucklas behind. The railway line continues along the other side of the valley. Follow this lane until you approach the outskirts of Heyop.

On the edge of this small hamlet, turn left to take the narrower lane, which begins on the level but slowly climbs into a valley. Continue past a couple of buildings on the left, and soon after the lane begins to climb steeply. Follow the lane uphill, passing a wood on your left, and you will find that the lane levels out once more, before it climbs the next steep section. Where an obvious gravel driveway bears off to the right, the lane makes for its final steep climb towards the summit, before gently dropping down to a junction with another lane.

From here, the views extend southwards towards Bache Hill, the highest point in the area at over 610m (2,000ft). Turn left here to follow this lane, which is also part of the Glyndwr's Way long-distance footpath that links Knighton with Welshpool via Machynlleth. The direction is still upwards, but the ascent is much gentler here. Some good views open out across the Teme Valley on the left as you amble along at a height of 366m (1,200ft). The lane then bears gently left and begins to climb again to the next summit, with views across to the Long Mynd and Titterstone Clee Hill ahead.

Knuclas viaduct

The lane begins to descend gently, passing a small lane on the right and then the entrance to Upper Dolwilkin Farm on your left. Bear right, around a small copse, and look out for glimpses of the Knucklas viaduct on your left. Soon the Glyndwr's Way footpath turns right across a field. However, you should stay on this lane as it rides this high viewpoint. Above Knucklas the earth mound that provided the foundation to Knucklas Castle can be seen on Castle Hill on your left.

The lane gently drops and bears right, and the wooded side of the Teme Valley around Knighton can be seen ahead. However, turn left on to a narrow lane that drops gently, before bearing left

and dropping steeply back down towards Knucklas. This lane is steep in places as it meanders downhill, but where it bears sharp right, stop to look ahead, for the view over the viaduct and the village is excellent here. Continue down the lane, passing a property on your left, then bear left in front of a bungalow, following this back to the outskirts of the village.

At a junction at the foot of the viaduct, turn right, go under the railway line, ignoring the lane on your right, to follow this lane back to the junction with the bridge. Bear right to return alongside Castle Inn, before turning right at the bus stop and back up the residential road to the railway station.

Looking back towards Heyop

POINTS OF INTEREST

- Knighton railway station, which is on the Heart of Wales Railway Line, is the only station in Britain where the town it serves is in a different country. Knighton is in Wales, but the station itself is in England, on the other side of the River Teme.
- The Church of St David at Heyop was rebuilt in 1880, although its parish registers date back as far as 1679.
- The Central Wales Railway Company extended the railway line from Knighton to Llandrindod between 1861 and 1865 and built the 13-arched viaduct at Knucklas.

OTHER WALKS IN THE AREA

The Offa's Dyke centre at Knighton provides a number of walking opportunities. Here Offa's Dyke and Glyndwr's Way meet, and there are several paths through and around Kinsley Wood on the outskirts of town.

Mortimer Forest

Ludlow is the administrative centre for south Shropshire, and many people regard it as the perfect English town. The architectural historian Nikolaus Pevsner described the main Broad Street as 'one of the most memorable streets in England'. The town is dominated by the huge tower of St Laurence's Church and the Norman fortress of Ludlow Castle, which now plays host to many festivals in this thriving community. However, step out of the confines of the town, across the banks of the sleepy River Teme, and you discover Mortimer Forest.

The forest is named after one of the dominant Norman families to have lived in the area, but the Forestry Commission now owns the land that once made up the larger Saxon forests of Mocktree, Deerfold and Bringewood. These woods would have provided fuel for the fires of the inhabitants of Ludlow and game for those in the castle. Today, the plantations provide numerous walking opportunities, and the views from the summit of High Vinnals are worth the climb. This walk leaves the centre of Ludlow using the Mortimer Trail and wanders into this predominantly Hereford-shire wood, meandering through Mary Knoll Valley to climb to High Vinnal's summit, before returning to Shropshire across Dinham Bridge with its imposing view of Ludlow Castle.

Walk category: invigorating | Length: about 16.5km (10½ miles) | Map: Explorer Sheet 203, Ludlow, Tenbury Wells and Cleobury Mortimer | Parking and starting point: Castle Square car park, Ludlow; other car parks are available; grid ref: SO 510 747 | Public transport: Whittle Buses service 435 links Shrewsbury to Ludlow (tel: 01584 872491); the Manchester–Cardiff railway serves Ludlow | Toilets: at Castle Square car park | Nearest tourist information: Ludlow

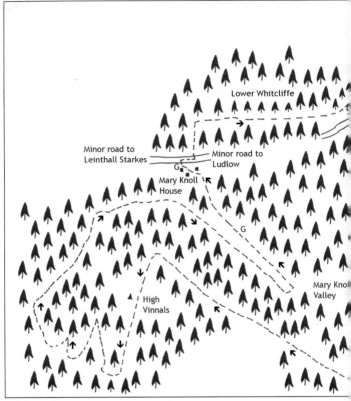

Map 22: Mortimer Forest

From the car park return to the market square and turn right towards the main entrance of Ludlow Castle. Turn right on to a signed footpath that leads around the edge of the castle, passing a Mortimer Trail information panel on your right. Continue around the castle walls, ignoring a path joining from the right, and where the path forks bear right, downhill, through a metal

Overleaf: the view from High Vinnals

barrier, to join a road. Climb up towards another road, and then turn right to cross over Dinham Bridge and the River Teme.

Once over the bridge, turn left to enter Whitcliffe Common and take the path ahead, signed as the Mortimer Trail, up some steps. Bear right to run parallel with the River Teme, before climbing more steps. Where the path forks, bear right on to a signed permissive path and follow this through the trees to a lane. Turn right on to this, downhill and where it bends sharp right, continue ahead on to a smaller lane called Lower Wood Road. Take the next path signed on your left.

Climb up. At a fork bear right on to another signed permissive path. This undulates through the Forestry Commission plantation. Ignore any small side paths to remain on this path until you reach a junction. Turn left to climb up to a road. Cross straight over with care and continue up the tarmac entrance to the Forest Enterprise offices and car parks. At a tarmac crossroad, continue straight ahead on to a forest track, signed as a permissive path. Note that this is still waymarked as the Mortimer Trail. Continue past a metal barrier and ignore any sidetracks to remain on this wide track through the trees. Soon the track reaches a clearing and then turns left and descends. Follow

Ludlow Castle

this as it drops, and where there is a field in front of you, bear right, as signed, to continue downhill. Views of Titterstone Clee hill can be glimpsed through the trees here. Stay on this track as it veers sharp right and continues to drop, and as you approach a house (only the roof is visible) the track turns sharp left. Don't turn left, but take the second turning on your right, which is a smaller path.

This path continues to drop, bearing round to the left before turning up to a wide track. Turn left on to this track and then, soon after, turn right uphill on to another signed permissive path.

After this levels out, the path bears right. At a crossing track turn right, uphill, through the trees.

Continue straight over a wide forest track to climb, following a wider path. Ignore a track on your left to continue upwards on a signed bridleway. There are good views along here and behind you. Where the path forks, bear right to continue ahead in the same direction. At the next junction, turn right and then left, as signed, where the track forks. Follow this uphill, around to the left, towards the summit. Ignore a path joining from the left, but opposite is a short track to a perfectly positioned bench, next to a deer hide, with excellent views across Herefordshire and Wales, including the Black Mountains to your left. This is a good place to stop for some refreshments.

From the bench return to the main path and turn right to proceed along the top of High Vinnals, before dropping down. A track joins from the left, but continue to descend. At a junction with another forest track turn right (leaving the Mortimer Trail) and follow the track around to the right, where it forks. Bear right to continue on the main forest track. Follow this track downhill, bearing sharp left and then zigzagging down to a junction with another forest track, where there is a small pond on your right. Turn right to proceed along this wide track as it gently climbs.

At the next junction bear right to continue climbing to another junction with a pond on your left. Turn left to go downhill. Soon you will see an 'all ability trail' signed on the left. Turn right opposite the sign, taking a wide forest track (not the smaller one) and follow this as it descends through deciduous trees. Ignore any small tracks on your left and right and follow this main track for about 1.6km (1 mile) to a large crossing track. Turn left, to cross over a stream, and then turn left again, to double back along the other side of the valley.

Ignore the steep path on your right and continue ahead, alongside the stream. When the track bears sharp right continue ahead on to a smaller path uphill. Go through a metal gate to climb up alongside a fence to another metal gate. Go through this and then bear right, as signed, climbing uphill towards Mary Knoll House. Follow the path past an outbuilding on your left and turn left on to a track that leads to the road. Go through a metal gate, and then turn right along the road. Take care along this short section. Turn left into the trees on a signed bridleway, drop down through the trees and cross straight over a crossing track to continue down. At the next forest track turn right to follow this through the trees, back to the lay-by opposite the entrance to the

Forest Enterprise offices. Turn left to rejoin the Mortimer Trail and follow this back down to the small lane. Turn right on to this and at the junction with the other lane, bear left and follow this downhill, and then round to the right, before turning left to cross back over Dinham Bridge. Don't turn left once you are over the other side, but instead continue up the narrow road and around the other side of Ludlow Castle so that you return to Castle Square.

POINTS OF INTEREST

- *Ludlow has over 500 Grade II listed buildings and the highest density of Michelin starred restaurants outside of London.*
- *Between 1473 and 1689 Ludlow Castle was the headquarters of the Council of the Marches, the administrative organisation governing Wales and the border counties.*
- *The original bridge over the River Teme at Dinham was built by Thomas Telford. The arch of the bridge on the Ludlow side is a remnant from Telford's bridge.*

OTHER WALKS IN THE AREA

The Mortimer Trail is a 48km (30 mile) route linking Ludlow with Kington in Herefordshire. Created in 1996, this popular route travels through some of the most unspoilt areas of the Welsh borders. There are numerous other waymarked walks starting from the Forestry Commission car parks at High Vinnals and Whitcliffe, and the River Teme has good paths on its journey around Ludlow.

Overleaf: swans on the River Wye

South Borders

There are five reservoirs in the Elan Valley, four of which were created between 1892 and 1903, and the fifth in the 1950s, all to supply water to Birmingham, some 120.7km (75 miles) away. As one drives around the lakeside roads now, these large stretches of water appear to enhance the local countryside, making it even more breathtaking. The Victorians took pride in their large engineering projects, something that can be seen today by the style and grandeur of the dams themselves. As a result, the concrete Claerwen Dam, constructed in the 1950s, was dressed up to look like its older brothers and sisters further down the valley.

After plentiful rain the water spills over the top of the dams with dramatic effect, something you are more likely to see in winter. This walk begins near the foot of the Caban Coch dam and then climbs up through woodland to the top of the dam and along the water's edge. It then heads away from the water, passing the historical remains of Nant y Gro dam, up to the surrounding hills, where there are fine views over the reservoir, before dropping down into the Dulas Valley. Finally, it climbs out of this, across the boggy mound of Carn Gafallt, to drop into the Elan Valley once more to return upstream to the visitor centre.

Walk category: invigorating | Length: about 11.5km (7¼ miles) | Map: Explorer Sheet 200, Llandrindod Wells and Elan Valley | Parking and starting point: Elan Valley visitor centre; grid ref: SN 928 646 | Public transport: none; nearest services are at Rhayader | Toilets: at visitor centre, mid-March to November, 7 days a week | Nearest tourist information: Elan Valley visitor centre or Rhayader

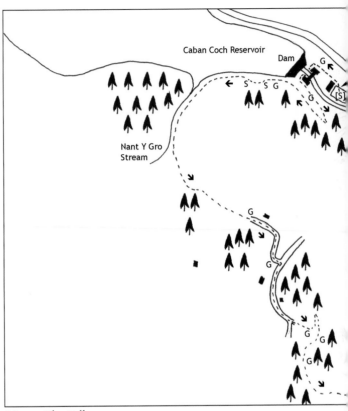

Caban Coch Reservoir

Dam

Nant Y Gro Stream

Map 23: Elan Valley

From the car park by the visitor centre head towards the centre building but bear right around it to pick up a turning area used by coaches and buses. Turn left and follow this track towards the dam, passing the sculpture celebrating Radnor in the year 2000. The track becomes stony and approaches a white metal gate. Go through the smaller wooden gate, as waymarked, and continue

Overleaf: Path beside reservoir

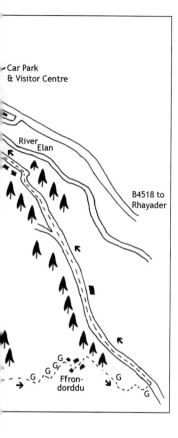

Car Park
& Visitor Centre

River Elan

B4518 to Rhayader

Ffron-dorddu

ahead, passing the waterworks building on your left. At the end of this, turn left, and then left again to follow the path as it crosses the River Elan by way of the stone bridge. At the other side, turn right and then left to go around the building, turning left again to pick up a wide track.

Follow the track, heading downstream to a large wooden gate. Go through the smaller gate on the left and continue as waymarked, climbing gently through the trees. Look out for the many information panels that Welsh Water has installed along here. Where the track forks, bear right to go uphill and shortly after turn sharp right at a junction with another track to continue climbing gently. Follow this track, ignoring a track that joins you later on the left. As you approach a wide metal gate, you will see that you are now level with the top of the dam. Go through the gate and take time to explore the viewpoint on the right, which overlooks the dam and reservoir.

To continue the walk follow the obvious path ahead, passing some iron railings on the left and a picnic area. This wide path veers towards the cliffs before gently edging closer to the water's edge. Soon the path narrows and then drops down to the edge of the reservoir and becomes very stony and more difficult to walk on. Stay on this path as it wanders along the bank, but bear left up some steps as waymarked. Cross the stile and turn right to run alongside the fence. Soon the waymarks send the path up to the left, where it levels out once more, to cross over a small stream before dropping down to another stile. Cross this and follow the path around to the left, where it becomes grassier.

The path turns its back on the reservoir and then bears left, as waymarked, to climb uphill. This gets steep in places. On the right you will pass an information panel, a stone shell and the remains of a dam in the trees. This is the Nant y Gro dam, where Barnes Wallis learned how much of a destructive force was needed to blow up a dam. From here he went on to create the bouncing bomb, famously tested on the reservoirs in Derbyshire before being used in the Second World War to destroy German dams in the Ruhr Valley.

Continue to climb steeply, with a tree plantation on the right, and remain on this obvious grass path as it climbs. Go over a crossing track and then bear left, heading towards a stand of coniferous trees ahead. As the path levels, bear left at the waymark and follow it, passing another small tree plantation on your right. This path then becomes an obvious track across open land. Ignore the bridleway that joins from the right and continue climbing gently, as signed, on a path that soon levels. It then begins a long descent, dropping down and zigzagging towards a metal gate. Ignore the track on the right but go through the metal gate on to a tarmac lane. This is narrow and drops steeply in places, but there are some good views through the Dulas Valley to the right. Continue past a stone building on the left, after which the lane begins to level. Follow this as waymarked, with fields on both sides, through a metal gate and then turn left to climb gently up to a junction with another lane. Turn right.

Stay on this lane, passing the entrance to Perthillwydion on your right before beginning to climb again. Just after a property on your left, turn left on to the wide signed bridleway that climbs

Caban Coch Dam

uphill. Go straight over the wide crossing track, through another gate and then bear round to the left. The track zigzags before straightening out and climbing more gently through the trees.

When you reach another large metal gate, go through and continue to climb until you reach another gate. Pass through this to enter Open Access land. Stay on this wide track as it bears gently left and then levels out. There are some good views on the right towards the Wye Valley.

Look out for a waymark post on your right. This is actually a crossing point where another bridleway cuts across from right to left, although it doesn't look it on the ground. Turn left here, on to what looks like a sheep track. This climbs up between two hillocks and may be boggy in places. As it levels out, bear gently right and then left over a small ridge. From this point the town of Rhayader can be seen a little off to the right. Straight ahead stands a metal gate beside some trees. Follow this path around to this and then go through. The bridleway now picks up a wide

Elan Valley

track once more and begins to descend, with a tree plantation on the left. Soon the track runs between two lines of trees and, later, between two fences. Where the track enters a new field, bear left to follow it around a tree line as it continues to drop. Bear right and go through a gate. Shortly afterwards the track turns left, downwards, and near the bottom leaves the trees to enter an open field with a fence on your right.

The track crosses through a stream and then turns left to go through a large metal gate. Once through, the track continues to drop, soon turning left to reach another gate. Continue through this and keep left as waymarked to go through several gates used as a sheep sorting area. Make sure that any gates you

open are securely closed behind you. Continue past the farm-house on your left, eventually bearing right out of the farm on to a tarmac track. Turn left to follow this downhill, and then turning sharp right, with good views over the Elan Valley now on your left. Where the tarmac driveway turns sharp left, the bridleway continues ahead as a wide farm track with a fence on your right. Follow this through a metal gate and continue between hedges, dropping down, bearing left and then right. This track begins to level out, and where there is a field entrance ahead bear left to stay on the track with hedges on both sides. Go through another metal gate, and you will eventually reach a tarmac lane.

Turn left and follow this back up the valley towards the dam. You will pass the tarmac entrance to Ffrondorddu (the farm you've just come through) on the left and then Cae-melyn bungalow on your right. The lane crosses a cattle grid and shortly after reaches a junction with another lane. Turn right and go downhill, crossing another cattle grid. Follow this quiet road as it zigzags its way back to Elan village.

The lane crosses over a small stream and continues between some white railings before it turns sharp right, over a bridge, straddling the River Elan. Once on the other side, turn left to return to the car park and visitor centre.

POINTS OF INTEREST

- *An aqueduct transfers the water from Elan Valley to the Frankley Reservoir in Birmingham. It is not pumped: gravity takes the water on its 120km (75 mile) journey.*
- *On average rain falls on the Elan estate on 235 days of the year.*
- *The poet Percy Bysshe Shelley moved into Nantgwyllt House on the banks of the River Claerwen with his new wife, Harriet Westbrook, in 1812, and hoped to buy the imposing property. Unfortunately, they couldn't secure the sale, and Nantgwyllt, along with several other dwellings, was lost forever when the valley was flooded.*

OTHER WALKS IN THE AREA

Much of the land around the Elan Valley is designated as Open Access land (visit www.ccw.gov.uk for detailed information), and the Elan estate encourages public access on its land. The visitor centre has numerous leaflets with waymarked trails and walks of various lengths, and a good footpath system means that it is possible to walk about many of the reservoirs.

Llandrindod Wells

The Victorian influences on Llandrindod Wells become obvious as soon as you enter the town. Large three- and four-storey buildings dominate the main roads, and the atmosphere has a definite flavour of a Victorian seaside resort. The town was a popular tourist destination during the 19th century, catering for up 80,000 visitors a year, all attracted by the fresh air and the spa waters of the numerous local springs. The arrival of the railway in 1865 coincided with the discovery of a new spring near the centre of town, resulting in the construction of new pump rooms and bathhouses. If you turn up in the last week of August you will think you've stepped back in time, as this is when the annual Victorian festival takes place.

This walk allows you to explore the centre of town before you escape to its outskirts and its lake and then on to the summit of Beacon Hill. From here, the walk drops through some quiet wooded glades to reach Shaky Bridge (which isn't), and crosses the River Ithon to reach St Michael's Church, which, curiously, is situated in the middle of a field.

Walk category: moderate | Length: about 9.5km (6 miles) | Map: Explorer Sheet 200, Llandrindod Wells and Elan Valley | Parking and starting point: car park next to Llandrindod Wells railway station; grid ref: SO 059 613 | Public transport: Heart of Wales Railway Line; bus service 704 (Newtown–Brecon) Monday to Saturday (tel: 01452 527516) | Toilets: next to railway station | Nearest tourist information: Llandrindod Wells

Depending on which way along the railway line you arrive or which car park by the station you use (there is one on both sides),

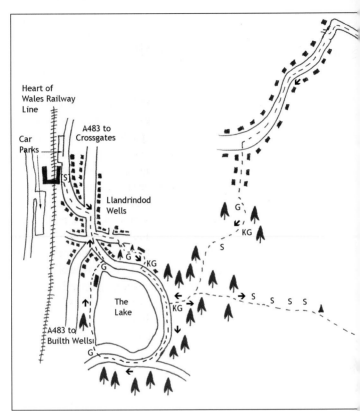

Map 24: Llandrindod Wells

aim for Station Crescent, which is on the same side of the railway line as platform 1. Turn right along Station Crescent, immediately passing some public toilets on your right, and then climb uphill as the road bears round to the left, passing the Royal Mail depot on the left and shops on your right. At the junction with the main road, turn right and then cross over this road at the zebra crossing and continue in the same direction. You'll soon pass the war memorial on your left, followed by the Metropole Hotel. At the corner of this

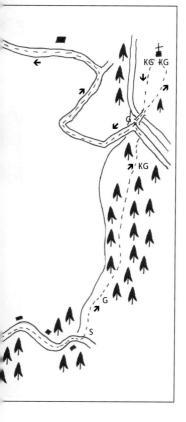

road, Temple Street, turn left uphill, passing St John's Church offices of Powys County Council on your left, and the college shortly after. Cross over Beaufort Road on your left, and then turn right, as signed, across this main road towards the main entrance to more Powys County Council offices. Just before you reach the main entrance, you'll see a path on your right, signed as a foot-path, with two bollards. Take this.

Follow this stone path through the trees to a junction. Turn right to go past a gate, then turn immediately left on to a path with a hedge running along your left. You may glimpse the council offices between the trees here. Continue along this path, over a wooden bridge, until you reach a junction with a tarmac path. Turn right, and fol-low this to a kissing gate. Go through the gate and turn left on to a tarmac pedestrian path with the road and lake on your right.

Continue along here until you reach a kissing gate on your left, beside a larger gate and an information panel for Llandrindod Lake Park. Go through on to a wide tarmac track that heads into the trees. This climbs gently and where it forks, bear right off the tarmac track to continue heading uphill through the trees. The path soon emerges into a clearing, becomes grassier and continues to climb.

The lake at Llandrindod Wells

At a junction of signed paths, turn left on to a signed footpath with a fence on your left and a hedge on your right. Follow this along the field edge. Just before you reach a stile in front of you, turn right, as signed, uphill. When you reach a small crossing track, turn left and at another junction with a small path, turn right. This continues to ascend. Ignore the small crossing tracks here and climb up into a clearing, where the path rises to meet a stile. Cross this and climb through the gorse bushes, as signed,

across the next field to another stile. Cross this and head over the field to yet another stile. Clamber over this and follow the grassy path as it rises more steeply to a fourth stile. Cross this and complete the final ascent to the triangulation point at the summit of Beacon Hill, about 355m (1,164ft). There are some fine 360-degree views from here across mid-Wales.

Drop down the other side of Beacon Hill to a stile, cross this and then turn left on to a narrow tarmac lane. Ignore the signed path on the right and instead continue along the lane as it drops down into the valley, with signed paths on the left and right near a property. Ignore these and follow the lane as it bears left, passing another signed path on the right, before crossing a stream, where the lane then becomes a track. Climb up and where this track bears right, turn left over a stile beside a metal gate on to a signed footpath. Follow this through a field to a large metal gate and go through.

The path enters a partly wooded area, which in spring is carpeted with bluebells. Soon the path runs close to the tree line on your left, with the stream below. Stay on the path as it meanders through the trees and then bears right, away from the stream, and climbs up to a clearing. From this summit the path drops down through a wide, open area to a kissing gate beside a large metal gate, on the outskirts of the woods. Go through and follow the path as it drops steeply to a parking area and picnic site beside a lane. Turn left on to the lane, and where this turns sharp left, turn right to go through a large gate, passing a sign welcoming you to St Michael's Church.

The path goes over Shaky Bridge, which is actually a concrete structure over the River Ithon, and enters a field. Climb up the obvious path that runs between trees, and as you re-enter the open field, if you look to your right, you will see the earthworks remains of Cefnllys Castle. However, turn left to reach the kissing gate into the grounds of St Michael's Church.

The path back takes the kissing gate opposite the main entrance to the church, and drops downhill in a straight line back to Shaky Bridge. Cross over, go through the gate and, at the lane, continue ahead and start to climb. Ignore the signed path and follow the lane as it becomes steeper and then turns sharp right. Climb past another stile on the right – there are good views here – and stay on the lane, turning sharp left and ignoring the dead-end lane ahead.

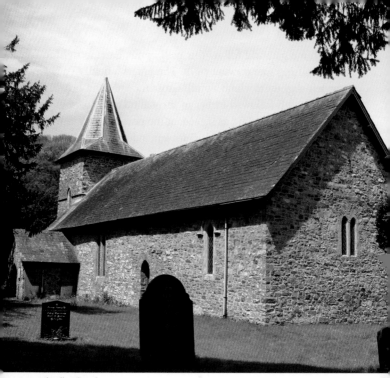

St Michael's Church

The lane, which is now relatively level, passes several signed paths on the left and right. Ignore these and continue past Bailey Einon Farm on your right, before you begin to drop down towards Llandrindod once more. Continue past the speed limit signs and follow the lane as it zigzags up, before continuing to descend. Pick up the tarmac pedestrian path on the left, ignoring side residential roads, and then cross over to the other side of the road to stay on the tarmac path. Drop downhill, and then turn left into Hillside Lane, which is also signed as a public footpath. This climbs gently between houses, but look out for a wooden gate on your left immediately before the main entrance to Hillside ahead. Go through the gate and follow this path uphill, bearing right to take a metal kissing gate on your right. This enters a field. At a signpost bear left slightly to climb uphill. Cross the stile and bear right to pick up a path followed earlier in the walk. Drop down alongside the fence, bearing right, as signed, at the next junction to reach the junction with the tarmac track. Turn left and follow this to the road.

Take care and cross straight over this. Turn left to take the pedestrian tarmac path around the lake. Follow it all the way round, passing several seats. Just as you pass the southern viewpoint, turn right through the large metal gates on to a wide path. This continues along the lake, before passing behind the lakeside café. Go through another set of gates to reach Princes Avenue, where you should turn left downhill. You will pass a children's play area on your left, but on the right are the remaining stones of Capel Maelog, believed to be one of the earliest Christian churches in mid-Wales.

Follow this road down to the Five Ways junction, cross over towards St John's Church offices again and walk along Temple Street, passing the Metropole Hotel on your right to return to the town centre and the railway station.

POINTS OF INTEREST

▪ *In Victorian times the rector of St Michael's Church was annoyed at having to trudge out from Llandrindod to undertake services here, so he removed the roof in an attempt to encourage parishioners to worship in the town.*

▪ *The Metropole Hotel is more decorative at the back than it is at the front because, when it was built, the developers thought that the main road through the town would go along that side of the building.*

▪ *Llandrindod Wells sits at 244m (800ft) above sea level.*

▪ *Castell Collen, a Roman fort, was built to the northwest of Llandrindod Wells, and there are finds from the site in the local museum.*

OTHER WALKS IN THE AREA

There are several leaflets available from the tourist information centre, including a 7.2km (4½ mile) circular walk to the nearby village of Howey and a linear walk to Newbridge-on-Wye.

WALK 25 | Water-Break-its-Neck

The Radnor Hills around New Radnor are some of the highest in this area, with Great Rhos, Black Mixen, Great Creigiau and Bache Hill all reaching heights above 610m (2,000ft). However, it's the Forestry Commission plantation of Warren Wood that this walk explores, because after heavy rainfall some of the excess rainwater from these peaks flows over the Water-Break-its-Neck waterfall in spectacular style.

This is a short walk and has been graded as 'easy' as a result, but you should note that there are a couple of sections that are quite steep, and you will certainly need stout footwear.

Walk category: easy | Length: about 5km (3 miles) | Map: Explorer Sheet 200, Llandrindod Wells and Elan Valley | Parking and starting point: picnic site, just off A44 near New Radnor; grid ref: SO 194 593 | Public transport: Sargeant Brothers service 461/462 (Llandrindod Wells–Kington–Hereford) serves New Radnor, Monday to Saturday (tel: 01544 230481) | Toilets: none | Nearest tourist information: Kington

There is a Forestry Commission car park quite close to the waterfall. For this walk, however, park by the picnic area, near the information board, just off the A44. From here, follow the wide track on foot, passing the information board on your left, as it heads into the valley and gently climbs. Take care here, because the occasional vehicle may pass along the track, but it is a relatively quiet spot. The views to the right over Vron Farm

Water-Break-its-Neck waterfall

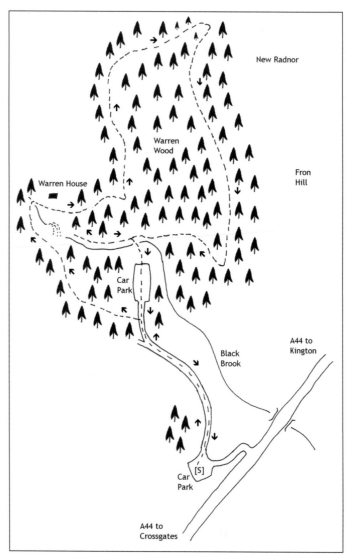

Map 25: Water-Break-its Neck

towards New Radnor are worth the extra walking effort along here. Ignore a bridleway that joins from the left and continue ahead. Where the track forks, bear right, towards where the Forestry Commission car park is signed, about 250m (820ft).

As you enter the car park, take the waymarked path on your left uphill, signed as the Water-Break-its-Neck trail. This climbs up through the trees to reach an area on your right where tantalising glimpses of the waterfall can be seen and certainly heard. Stay on the path as it continues to climb and then forks. Bear right, alongside a fence, and, where a small path joins from your left, continue ahead to drop down alongside the fence. The path turns right to cross over a stream near the top of the fall, and then turns left again and begins to climb.

Bear left towards a house and then right as waymarked, keeping the house on your left and the valley on your right. Follow the path, as signed, shortly after which it descends steeply between the trees. Take care on this section, particularly after rainfall. At the bottom of this section, turn left, as signed, and then drop down to a junction.

Turn left and climb uphill to reach a wide crossing track, which leads to Warren House. Cross straight over this to stay on the smaller path, as it climbs through a clear section of young trees, with the occasional glimpse of the surrounding hills. Soon the path levels out, before bearing gently right. Drop down on a grass path to a junction with a wide track. Turn left to climb uphill, but shortly after turn right on to a small path, and then turn sharp right again, as signed, doubling back on yourself, and drop downhill through the trees towards Black Brook. This section is quite steep in places. Cross over a wooden footbridge spanning Black Brook and turn right to stay on the path as it negotiates its way around a tree and begins to climb up the other side of the valley.

At a junction with a wide track turn right and follow the track as it undulates through the tree plantation. Before the track nears

Looking towards New Radnor

some fields on your left, turn right, as signed, on to a smaller track, which drops downhill, but soon rejoins the wide track, which is now stony. Turn right on to this track and drop down to re-cross Black Brook and climb up to a wide junction.

Continue straight over and follow the signed path to Water-Break-its-Neck. This 200m (656ft) path follows the water's edge closely, up and down steps and over duckboards to its foot. Return along the same path to reach the junction with the wide track.

Turn right on to this and follow it uphill, through the Forestry Commission car park, and back along the valley to return to the car park and picnic area.

POINTS OF INTEREST

■ *Victorian visitors to Llandrindod Wells would often undertake a day's excursion to see the waterfall, which is 76m (250ft) high.*

■ *Hen harriers may be seen flying above the trees, as well as buzzards and red kites.*

OTHER WALKS IN THE AREA

The hills above New Radnor can be explored under Open Access land arrangements, and several bridleways lead up into them, although care should be taken, particularly around Harley Dingle, which is clearly marked on OS maps as a Danger Area. Check the Open Access website for Wales for any other restrictions that may apply in this area. A popular trek across the hills from the same car park used in this walk takes the byway across the hills to the village of Llanfihangel Rhydithon, a linear walk of over 9.7km (6 miles).

Croft Castle and its beautiful church afford an opportunity to explore the gentle rolling hills of north Herefordshire, while still offering some far-reaching views. The country house has family connections that date back to the Norman Conquest, but on the nearby hill summit of Croft Ambrey are the earthwork remains of an Iron Age hill fort.

This gentle walk explores Bircher Common, which is also owned by the National Trust and designated as Open Access land, and provides wonderful views across Herefordshire and Wales, stretching as far as the Black Mountains and the Brecon Beacons. There is also plenty of time to explore the castle and its grounds.

Walk category: easy | Length: about 8.5km (5¼ miles) | Map: Explorer Sheet 203, Ludlow, Tenbury Wells and Cleobury Mortimer | Parking and starting point: National Trust car park at Croft Castle, open all year, dawn until dusk; grid ref: SO 453 656 | Public transport: none | Toilets: available for users of the tea room (check www.nationaltrust.org.uk for opening times) | Nearest tourist information: Leominster

---

From the castle car park head downhill, walking parallel with the driveway to reach a gate beside a cattle grid. Go through the gate and turn left on to a track that bears left and drops downhill. At the junction with a larger stone track, turn sharp right into Fishpool Valley. Continue to drop downhill, passing a large pond on your left and ignoring the path on your left immediately after it.

Where the track forks bear left to remain on the stone track until you reach another pool on your left. Take the next small

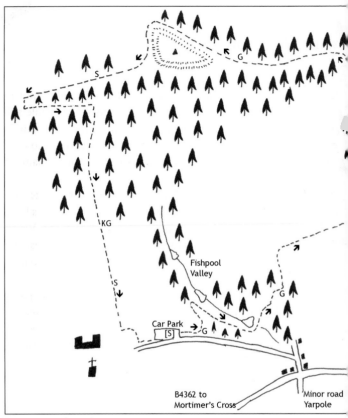

Map 26: Croft Castle

path on the left, which allows you to pass along the head of the pool and over a stream, before beginning to climb up through the trees. At a junction with a small path, continue ahead uphill, and then turn right at the next junction to reach a large wooden gate.

Go through the gate to enter a clearing and turn left on to a wide stone track that leads uphill. Just before the track bears left to a gate back into the woods, you should bear right towards

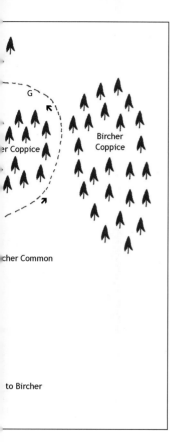

G

Bircher
Coppice

er Coppice

cher Common

to Bircher

some wooden posts and on to the open expanse of Bircher Common. Note that there may be horses and other livestock grazing here.

To begin with, bear right and head across the common, towards the right-hand side of Oaker Coppice higher up on the hill. To your right are good views across Herefordshire. As the coppice on your left draws nearer, veer up towards its outside edge so that its boundary fence is on your left, and then follow this round to the left. Soon an obvious track appears. Follow this as you continue to bear left, but where you see a waymark identifying the Mortimer Trail, bear left away from this track, to pick up a smaller path, which is closer to the boundary fence of Oaker Coppice.

As this smaller path continues through the trees between the enclosures of Oaker and Bircher Coppices, cross over a stone track that leads to an entrance to Oaker Coppice on your left. Continue ahead through the trees and where the fence on your left bears sharp left, a clearing opens up in front of you. Head into this clearing and bear around the right-hand side of the small hillock and an obvious path, signed as the Mortimer Trail, will appear. This leads into the trees, but don't take it. Instead, take a

Looking into Wales from Croft Ambrey

small wooden gate on the right. Go through this and bear left to follow the edge of Croft Wood on your left. Stay on this level path, ignoring a signed path on the right that drops downhill. Views of north Herefordshire and south Shropshire can be glimpsed through the trees.

The path drops briefly, passing a gate on the left, and then climbs again to continue on the level with a fence on the left. Continue ahead through a large wooden gate, and soon the path

bears left to a perfectly positioned seat and a great viewpoint that looks across mid-Wales.

From here, the path, signed as the Mortimer Trail, drops down, and it then bears around to the right. Ignore the gate on the left and continue along the grass path, crossing over a stile. At a junction of paths, turn left uphill to reach a junction with a wide track. Turn left into the trees and follow this, ignoring a track that joins from the right, until you reach a large crossing track. Turn

The path around Croft Ambrey

right and follow this downhill. Where this track veers left, continue ahead through a kissing gate and then drop down through a field, following the left-hand boundary edge to reach another gate. Cross over the stile next to this and follow the track back towards Croft Castle and its car park.

POINTS OF INTEREST

■ *Croft Castle has one of the finest restored walled gardens and vineyards in Herefordshire.*
■ *Croft Ambrey Iron Age hill fort is believed to have begun life as a settlement around 1050 bc.*

■ *Sir Richard Croft is buried in St Michael's Church, next to Croft Castle. He led troops from here into battle at Mortimer's Cross in Herefordshire in 1461 during the Wars of the Roses.*

OTHER WALKS IN THE AREA

The Mortimer Trail is a 48km (30 mile) route linking Ludlow with Kington, but there are several circular loop walks that link up with it. One such route is the Wigmore Loop, which creates a 16km (10 mile) circular walk linking Croft Ambrey Hill fort with the village of Wigmore.

WALK 27 | Hergest Ridge

Kington nestles in the valley of the River Arrow, which wends its way from nearby Gwaunceste Hill in Wales to meet the River Lugg near Leominster. To the north of this river, and the west of the town, stands Hergest Ridge. Reaching 426m (1,397ft), it is one of the largest hills in the immediate vicinity and is a popular spot for locals as well as tourists who venture up for the views. On a clear day, they won't disappoint, encompassing Corn Du and Pen Y Fan to the southwest, the Black Mountains, round to the Malvern Hills in the east and Titterstone Clee Hill to the north-east.

This walk takes you through the busy market town of Kington and then follows the Arrow Valley to Hergest Bridge, where it begins its ascent to the top of the ridge, before following Offa's Dyke on its long descent back down into the town.

Walk category: invigorating | *Length: about 12km (7½ miles)* | *Map: Explorer Sheet 201, Knighton and Presteigne* | *Parking and starting point: Mill Street car park, Kington; grid ref: SO 295 565* | *Public transport: Sargeant Brothers service 461/462 (Kington–Hereford), Monday to Saturday (tel: 01544 230481)* | *Toilets: Mill Street, next to Kington Museum* | *Nearest tourist information: Kington*

From Mill Street car park head towards the school and then turn right down Mill Street, passing the tourist information centre on your right and the Kington Museum, Coach House and toilets on your left. At the junction with the main road turn right into the

St Mary's Church, Kington

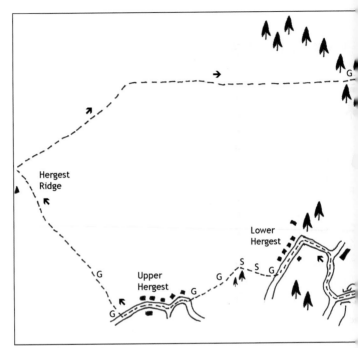

Map 27: Hergest Ridge

High Street. Follow this main road as it turns sharp right into Bridge Street, passing the Baptist church on the left, to continue over the stone bridge across the River Arrow. Turn right into Kingswood Road and climb gently.

Before you reach the speed restriction signs turn right on to a tarmac lane to Newburn Farm, also signed as a footpath. Follow this, catching occasional glimpses of the town over the top of the hedgerow on your right. Before you reach the farm, look out for two gates together on your left, which lead into different fields. The footpath turns left here, as signed, through the second gate, and heads across the field to the next large metal gate in a wooden fence. Take care, because there may be horses in any of these

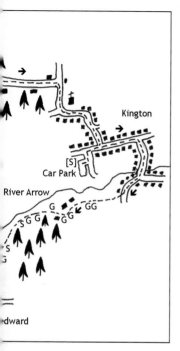

fields. Go through this gate and cross straight over the field to another gate, and after you have passed through this, bear right on to a concrete drive. Follow this round to your left, between farm buildings and some cottages. Continue to pass some stables on your right to reach another metal gate. Go through and follow the path along the right-hand field edge to a gate in the corner. Once on the other side, the path continues between trees to drop down to another gate.

Go through this and fork right, as waymarked on the tree ahead, along the top of a bank, before gently dropping down through the trees into a field until you reach a bridge. Do not cross this, but turn left, uphill, to a stile. Cross this and follow the path, as signed, along the right-hand field edge. Continue through the tree line into the next field to reach a stile on the right of a metal gate on the other side. Cross this and continue along the field edge until the boundary turns sharp right away from you, from where you should continue ahead to reach a gate in the next hedge. Go through this and bear left, climbing uphill, to a stile that soon becomes visible in the trees ahead. Cross over and drop down some steps to reach a narrow tarmac lane.

Turn right and follow this lane downhill as it meanders around a property on your left before picking up the River Arrow again on your right. At a junction with a larger road, turn right, cross

Remains of Castle Twts near Lower Hergest

over Hergest Bridge and the river and follow this for a short distance. Ignore the signed path on your left and take the next narrow lane on the left, opposite the entrance to Hergest Court. Ignore the signed path on the left here and continue on the lane, as it climbs steeply, signed to Lower and Upper Hergest.

The remains of a castle can be seen on your right from a footpath where the lane turns sharp left. To stay on the route follow the lane as it turns left and wanders past the picturesque

cottages of Lower Hergest. The lane gently drops, before climbing again and passing a footpath on your left. Take the next signed footpath on your right into a field, which may contain livestock. Go through a large metal gate and climb up to the diagonally opposite field corner. Cross over a stile and continue in the diagonal direction towards the nearest edge of a small conifer plantation. As you reach this, turn right to reach a large wooden stile.

Cross over to enter another field and turn left. Follow the left-hand boundary to reach a large metal gate. Go through this to join a wide farm track, which drops down from your right and then continues ahead on level ground, with some great views across to the Black Mountains to your left. Continue along here, until the track drops down to a large metal gate. Go through this to pick up the narrow tarmac lane again. Turn right and follow this through the pretty hamlet of Upper Hergest. Ignore the small lane to your left and instead follow the lane you are on round to the right, where it soon begins to climb gently. With Upper Hergest behind you, take the next signed bridleway on your right, through a large metal gate, and climb uphill between fences.

This climbs steeply up to another metal gate. Go through this and enter the open heathland of Hergest Ridge. Bear left gently, away from the tall, obvious signpost, and look for a shorter waymark post. From here, climb uphill as waymarked on a wide, grass path between the gorse bushes. After a short while the route bears left to continue on a wide, grass track. Continue to climb, passing another waymark post. There are good views behind you of the Black Mountains, and in the distance, to the right of these, you might be able to make out the flat tops of Pen Y Fan and Corn Du.

The path then passes another waymark post before it bears right, passing a pile of large stones on the right and continuing to climb. Stay on this path, heading for another waymark post, which soon becomes visible. When you reach this bear left, as directed, to walk between the highest point of Hergest Ridge on your left, and the triangulation point on the right, towards another tall waymark.

Drop down now, over a crossing track and through an area of gorse to reach another wide crossing track. Turn right and follow this – there are great views to your right and left. This wide, grass path passes a small pool on the right, shortly after which the Offa's Dyke long-distance path joins from the left. Continue in the same direction, and cross over a large crossing track, which is actually the remains of a disused racecourse, on to a track that is now waymarked with the acorn symbol of the Offa's Dyke National Trail. Follow this through the gorse, and then pass a small plantation on your right. Cross over a signed footpath, following Offa's Dyke as it begins its long descent downhill.

Another wide, grass track joins from the left. Shortly after, continue straight over another large crossing track (which is the other end of the disused racecourse). Glimpses of Kington can be seen ahead. With a bank of gorse on your right, the path drops down to a point where three large tracks merge together to continue heading downhill. Ignore the signed footpath on your left and remain on Offa's Dyke. Where this forks, bear right on to the wider section, which soon becomes a stone track, and drops down to a large wooden gate.

Go through the gate and join a narrow tarmac lane. Follow this downhill, passing Hergest Croft Gardens on your right and the visitor car park on the left. Ignoring any signed paths on the left and right, follow the lane downhill to pick up a pedestrian path on the right, until your reach the junction with a main road. Turn right towards Kington town centre, crossing over Hergest Road on the right, and follow this main road sharp left with St Mary's Church on your left. Cross over to the other side of the road to continue on the pedestrian path as it bends right and begins to drop downhill. Cross Doctor's Lane on your left to pass the Royal Oak Inn on your right and the Swan Hotel on the left. When you reach the junction at the bottom of the hill, turn right into Mill Street to return to the car park.

POINTS OF INTEREST

■ *Sir Arthur Conan Doyle had family connections with the area and was a frequent visitor. It is believed that the eerie stories of Black Vaughan, the ghost in the shape of a large black dog, may have inspired his 1902 novel,* The Hound of the Baskervilles.

■ *After the success of his first album, Tubular Bells, the musician and composer Mike Oldfield retreated to the Kington area to work on his second album, which he called Hergest Ridge.*

■ *Kington's Golf Course on Bradnor Hill is the highest in England.*

OTHER WALKS IN THE AREA

As well as having the Offa's Dyke long-distance path travel through the town, Kington is also at the end of the Mortimer Trail, a 48km (30 mile) route linking Kington with Ludlow in Shropshire. This is a beautiful two-day trek, with several waymarked loops, one of which is at nearby Titley. Several other circular walks can be taken from the town, using Hergest Ridge to Gladestry and to Bradnor Hill, which is owned by the National Trust.

This quiet village lies on the banks of the River Edw, a tributary of the River Wye, near Builth Wells. It's a tranquil place, although the Seven Stars Inn is popular because of its good reputation for food. People have been coming to Aberedw since the Norman times, as is evidenced by the motte that remains nearby. However, if you wander up on to Llandeilo Hill, where the best viewpoints are to be found from the rocky outcrops, the chances are that you won't see a soul. Much of this area is designated as Open Access land.

This walk follows the River Edw upstream, passing some beautiful picnic spots before climbing out of the valley bottom and then steeply up on to Llandeilo Hill. During the descent from Aberedw Rocks the views down the Wye Valley stretch towards the Brecon Beacons and the Black Mountains. The walk then runs alongside the B4567 with the River Wye down to the left. Unfortunately, little remains along this section of the railway line that used to run from Rhayader all the way to Hay-on-Wye.

Walk category: invigorating | Length: about 12km (7½ miles) | Map: Explorer Sheet 188, Builth Wells | Parking and starting point: park in Aberedw village; grid ref: SO 078 474 | Public transport: Roy Brown's Coaches runs one bus, Mondays only (tel: 01982 552597) | Toilets: none | Nearest tourist information: Builth Wells

---

There is no designated car parking area in the village of Aberedw, so park safely and considerately on the roadside. Follow the road into the village, passing the Seven Stars Inn on your right, and then drop downhill. Where the road forks by a telephone box,

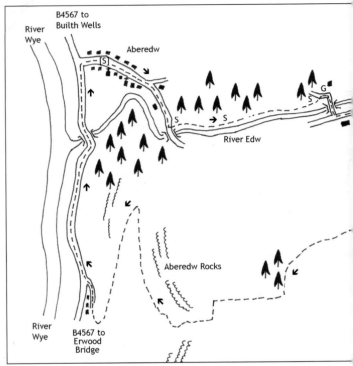

Map 28: Aberedw

bear right and climb uphill, eventually leaving the village behind you. The lane then drops once more, down towards a bridge over the River Edw, but before you reach this, bear left, over a stile, on to a signed footpath into a field. Cross straight over the field to reach another stile, climb over this and follow the path with a fence and the river on your right.

Continue ahead on to a large track, which joins from the left, and follow this as it meanders through small riverside meadows. The path then climbs up into a wooded area before dropping down into a wide, open field, which may contain livestock.

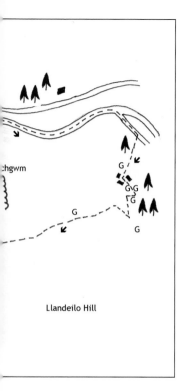

chgwm

G

G G

G

G G

G

Llandeilo Hill

Follow the path through this field and then through a narrow fenced section, as waymarked, into the next field. The path stays close to the right-hand field edge, but once you reach the other side ignore the wide metal gate ahead and turn left to continue around the field boundary, turning right where the fence does the same. Climb up to a stile, cross over and drop down to a tarmac lane.

Turn right here and go through the large metal gate. Follow the road round to the right. Ignore the signed path on the left and continue over the bridge across the River Edw to reach a junction with a quiet lane. Turn left and follow this lane upstream. There are wide grass verges and, within a short distance, a couple of picnic tables. Near a small waterfall the lane begins to climb, passing through a quarried area, before dropping back down again to continue over a cattle grid. Follow the lane past Glan Edw on your left and then round to your right. Once again, the lane climbs. Shortly after crowning this summit, turn right through a large metal gate signed as Pentwyn Farm. (This bridleway is not waymarked.)

Climb up, and once you have passed between two wooden posts where a gate once hung, bear right, off the track, to follow the hedge line straight uphill towards some conifer trees. Rejoin

Lush hills of the Edw Valley

the farm track and turn right, through a large metal gate, and follow the track as it veers around to the left, through several gates, uphill, and through a final gate before it begins to drop. Stay on this track as it runs alongside a field on the left and then climb up to a junction.

Turn sharp right, uphill, through a large metal gate and then follow the track, as it turns left and continues to climb. Where it begins to level, you will see a large metal gate ahead, and a grass track forking right uphill. At this point, turn sharp right, to double back on yourself, and go around a small enclosure or sheep pen. This path is not visible on the ground, but head diagonally downhill towards the fence, possibly through livestock, and at the

fence, turn left. Follow this to the end of the field to reach a large metal gate. Go through the gate to enter the open hillside of Llandeilo Hill, which is Open Access land. Continue ahead, bearing left slightly, to pick up a grass path through the bracken.

This path continues to bear left, climbing gently up the side of Llandeilo Hill and offering some great views over the Edw Valley. This section of the route is a bit confusing because there are several sheep tracks crisscrossing the area, but because it is Open Access land it doesn't matter if you veer off-route slightly. Continue in the same general but gentle uphill direction. Marked on the OS map is a ditch, labelled as Sychgwm, that runs downhill. If you find you have to cross over this, you need to bear left

uphill at a greater angle. Ideally, you will walk past the top of this, higher up the hill.

Eventually, you will join a wide, grassy path. You should turn right and follow as it gently descends. The track then crosses a relatively level section before dropping more steeply. Ignore any crossing tracks or tracks that run parallel, and instead follow this track downhill to pick up a fence and field on your right. The track then bears left away from this and drops down to a point where another track joins from the right. The path now begins to climb again. Where it forks, bear left uphill. Follow this over a crossing track and climb up alongside some pylons on your right. The path zigzags its way up to the summit, to reach another crossing track.

Turn right on to this and follow it under the pylons as the wide, grassy track travels across a plateau. There are some good views of the Wye Valley to your left. The path then drops and bears gently to the right towards a craggy outcrop. At a junction with a crossing track, turn left and follow this to reach another crossing track. Turn right, as if heading towards the crags once again, continue over another crossing track and then drop down to your left. Where the path forks, bear right, down to a junction under the crags, and then turn left.

Follow this path until it forks, near a boundary stone. Bear right on to a grass path and follow this around to your right, under the crags and with views up the Wye Valley ahead. This path drops gently. Look out for a path that appears to come from a cleft between the rocks on your right and drops down to cross this path. Turn left here, doubling back on yourself slightly, and walk through the bracken to continue downhill. This path drops over several ridges and soon you should spot a small lane with houses down to your right.

The clear path drops down, continues over a small crossing track and then climbs briefly to reach a wider crossing track. Turn

The Wye Valley

right here and follow this down, and then round to the right, where it becomes a stone track. Continue in a downhill direction, passing houses on your left. Eventually bear left, over a cattle grid and between the stone remains of a railway bridge, to reach the B4567. Turn right. Follow the road with care because some locals use it instead of the A road on the other side of the River Wye, which is to your left. Follow this road as it zigzags down to cross over the River Edw, right where it meets the Wye, and then take the next lane on your right, signed to Aberedw. Climb up to return to the village and the start of the walk.

POINTS OF INTEREST

- *St Cewydd's Church in Aberedw dates from the 14th century, although it is believed that the site has been a place of worship since the 6th century.*
- *Welsh folklore suggests that Prince Llewelyn, the last prince of Wales, hid in caves near Aberedw before he was captured by the troops of King Edward I and later killed.*
- *The River Edw is popular with fishing enthusiasts looking for wild brown trout.*

OTHER WALKS IN THE AREA

An alternative circular walk heads north from the village, up on to Aberedw Hill and then back along the ridge between Milo Brook and Cwmblaenerw Brook, to Rhyscog, to return to Abweredw via quiet lanes. The Wye Valley walk follows the hills flanking the western side of the River Wye here, making possible a linear walk from Builth Wells to Erwood, and using bus service 704 (Brecon–Newtown) to make the return journey.

Queenswood Country Park sits on the western side of Dinmore Hill. The main A49 trunk road zigzags its way over the top, while the Manchester–Cardiff railway line tunnels through. Despite these modern intrusions, it's possible to see a variety of flora and fauna from this park as well as to enjoy some excellent views. Included within the country park are a 27 hectare (67 acre) arboretum, a redwood grove, an autumn garden and even an old orchard. With numerous waymarked trails, play areas, a tourist information centre, shop, café and toilets, this is a popular place throughout the year. The viewpoint offers panoramic views across south Herefordshire, stretching from the Malverns in the east to the Black Mountains in the west.

The walk allows you to explore some of the country park, including the viewpoint, but then leaves the park briefly to drop into the hamlet of Hope under Dinmore, with glimpses of views across north Herefordshire, before making its way back into the park. Look out for deer if you are really quiet, and listen for woodpeckers. Spring visitors are often overwhelmed by the number of bluebells that can be seen here.

Walk category: easy | Length: about 4.5km (2¾ miles) | Map: Explorer Sheet 202, Leominster and Bromyard | Parking and starting point: car park at Queenswood Country Park, Dinmore Hill, off A49; grid ref: SO 506 514 | Public transport: Lugg Valley Primrose Bus service 492 links Leominster to Hereford (tel: 01568 612759) | Toilets: next to shop at car park | Nearest tourist information: Queenswood Country Park

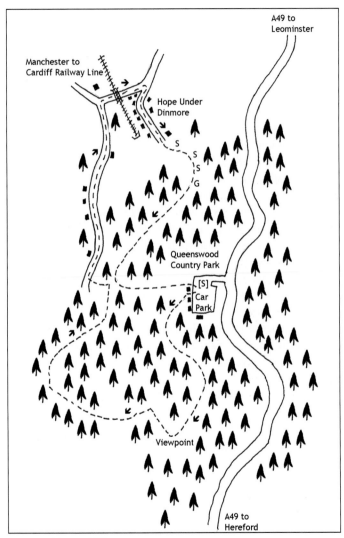

Map 29: Dinmore Hill

From the car park head between the two buildings containing the tourist information centre and toilets on your right and the café on your left. Bear left, past some picnic tables, to pick up a crushed gravel path, which is signed as the Sovereign Walk. This is also waymarked with the four main trails that negotiate the park. At the first junction bear left, waymarked as the Deer Trail and Fox Trail, and where this path forks again, bear left. Wander through the redwood grove and continue over a small ditch. Bear right to follow a path of wood chippings, which soon gives way to a bare earth path, until you reach a junction. Turn left here. Soon after, fork right, passing another sign for the Sovereign Walk.

Follow this path to reach a junction with Nutt's Ride. Cross straight over and then immediately bear right to join another wide track, waymarked as the Badger Trail. Ignore any side paths and follow this gently uphill, forking left to reach the viewpoint. There is a toposcope here, identifying the main peaks, and a telescope allowing a closer look.

With your back to the viewpoint, take the track to the left of the wooden benches and continue straight over a junction with a path to climb gently along a wide woodland path, passing the quarry on your right. Ignore a small path on your right and at a wider crossing track turn left towards a clearing. This brings you to the bottom end of Oak Avenue. Cross straight over this wide, grassy area on to a smaller path, which drops down through the trees and is now waymarked as the Fox Trail, until you reach a junction with four possible exits (not including the path you're on). Turn right on to a path waymarked as the Deer Trail, which is on level ground. Follow this around to the right, as signed, where the path then climbs uphill to reach another junction.

Turn left on to another level, wide track, still waymarked as the Deer Trail, and follow this, ignoring any side paths. The path bears to the right and meanders around the rear of the autumn garden, turning sharp right to reach a junction with a wide tarmac lane. Turn right and follow this with care, because a few vehicles use this route, keeping the autumn garden on your right. Soon you pass the old orchard with its reading seat signed on your left, which is worth exploring. Soon after a brick-pillared, metal gate on your left, fork left on to a small path, waymarked with the Deer and Fox Trail logos. Follow this along the tarmac lane, where it then bears left into the trees. Ignore the first path on your left, but take the next left immediately afterwards to stay on the waymarked route. Soon the Fox Trail turns right, but you should continue until you reach a junction of paths, with a wide track on your right.

Turn left on to a small path, which drops downhill, and continue over a small crossing track to emerge between some wooden posts on to a tarmac lane. Turn right on to this and follow it downhill. This quiet lane has views on the left overlooking some orchards and ahead over north Herefordshire and the Clee Hills in Shropshire. Continue past the cottages and ignore any signed footpaths, until you reach a junction with another lane. Turn right, pass under both rail bridges into Hope under Dinmore and, where the lane turns left, turn right, signed as a public footpath.

This track wanders between some cottages, eventually becoming a grass track that bears left. Cross over a stile and climb up some steps between two fences to reach another stile. Continue over this into a field and bear gently right to a third stile. Cross this and follow the path alongside a wire fence on your right. Climb up to a small wooden gate and go through it to re-enter Queenswood Country Park. Bear right, as signed, and at a crossing track go straight over and climb up to a wide, grass crossing track. Turn right to continue climbing uphill, bearing gently around to the left. When you reach a junction with a grass path, turn right. This soon leads to another crossing track. Continue ahead on a wide stone track, which climbs up, before levelling off. Ignore any side paths until you reach a junction of

Information centre at Queenswood

paths that you should recognise. Cross over, then bear left, signed as the Fox Trail, on to a small path that leads into a clearing. Cross through this to reach the tarmac lane. Continue over this and turn left, as signed, to return to the car parks and tourist information centre.

POINTS OF INTEREST

- *Both the café and tourist information buildings at Queenswood have been relocated. The café used to be in Hereford, and the tourist information centre came from Leominster.*
- *The arboretum at Queenswood was created in 1953 and has 500 exotic and rare species of trees and shrubs.*
- *The rail tunnel that runs under Dinmore Hill took 2½ years to build and used over 3 million bricks.*

Viewpoint at Queenswood Country Park

OTHER WALKS IN THE AREA

There are several waymarked trails around Queenswood Country Park that will allow you to explore the area further; ask for more details at the information centre. If you want a slightly longer route take the footpath south of Hope under Dinmore through Upper Buskwood farm and then past Friar's Grove to Westhope, before cutting back to Hope under Dinmore using the single-track lane, which also provides good views.

WALK 30 | Dorstone

The River Dore wanders gently through the Golden Valley, an idyllically quiet and beautiful area of Herefordshire and one that isn't troubled by A roads. With the grander Black Mountains bordering the area to the southwest and the meandering River Wye to the north, the landscape itself has helped to keep development at bay. The village of Dorstone lies close to the Welsh border, and the River Dore is little more than a small stream as it passes by.

This walk actually begins at Arthur's Stone, a Neolithic burial chamber high on a ridge above the village. There is parking here for only a couple of cars, although it is possible to pick up this walk from where the bus stops at Dorstone village green. The route ambles its way northwest to Merbach Hill, a small area of Open Access land with wide views across the Wye Valley and north Herefordshire, before wending its way back into the Golden Valley and down to the village of Dorstone, with its popular village pub. From here, the route climbs back up to Arthur's Stone.

Walk category: moderate | Length: about 8.75km (5½ miles) | Map: Explorer Sheet OL13, Brecon Beacons National Park, Eastern Area | Parking and starting point: limited parking next to Arthur's Stone; grid ref: SO 319 431 | Public transport: Stagecoach service 39 (Hereford–Brecon) serves Dorstone, Monday to Saturday (tel: 01633 485118) | Toilets: none | Nearest tourist information: Hay-on-Wye or Hereford

From the parking area by Arthur's Stone follow the lane to pass the burial chamber on your left. Where the lane bears right, take

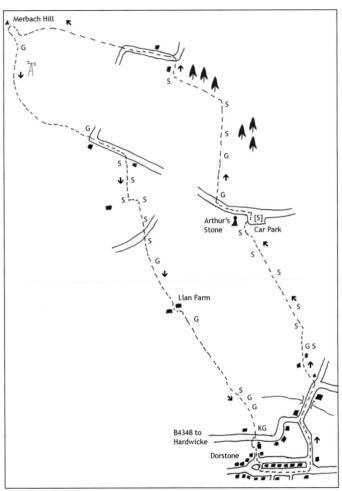

Map 30: Dorstone

the signed bridleway on your right, going through a double metal gate into a field and following its right-hand edge. At the end of this field go through a large metal gate and bear to the left of a stand of coniferous trees to reach the field corner. Ignore the metal gate on your left. Instead, cross the stile ahead to enter another field and drop down along the left-hand boundary, where there are some good views across Herefordshire ahead.

When you come to a stile in the hedge, cross over and then bear left as waymarked downhill, towards the edge of a wooded area. Look out for a large wooden gate in the boundary fence. Don't go through this, but drop down into a cutting, as signed, to follow the woodland boundary round to your right, dropping down between some trees to enter an open area. Continue to walk downhill to a stile, cross this and then a small wooden bridge and follow the path as it passes a property on your left. At a junction with a tarmac lane, turn left.

Follow this lane uphill, passing the entrances to several properties on your right, and then, where the lane turns sharp left, continue ahead on to a signed bridleway. This climbs gently between hedges and fields until it enters the more open area of Merbach Hill. You are now entering Open Access land. Continue ahead, over a crossing track, to remain on this path that becomes smaller as it meanders its way through the trees and areas of bracken. Eventually, you will notice that the path is beginning to climb, and in an open area of bracken it reaches a junction with a wider grass track. Turn left on to this and climb briefly, before levelling out.

At a smaller crossing track turn right and follow this path through what seems to be a quarried area to reach the triangulation point at the top of Merbach Hill. It is only 318m (1,043ft) above sea level, but below lies the Wye Valley with the river flowing from Hay-on-Wye on its journey to Hereford.

From the trig point follow the path around to your left, passing the quarried area once more, to reach a small wooden gate. Go through this to leave the Open Access land and enter a field, which may have livestock in it. Follow the contour of the hill, aiming for between the tree line on your right and the aerial on

The Wye Valley from Merbach Hill

the left. Once past the aerial, the path bears towards the tree line and then follows this boundary towards the end of the field. Before reaching this, it joins a stone track and then continues ahead to a large metal gate.

Go through the gate to join a tarmac lane. Continue ahead, passing a property on your right, and climb gently, but just before the next property on the right take the stile next to a metal gate to enter another field. Follow this path, as signed, along the left-hand field edge, down to another stile. Cross this to enter another

field and bear left to pick up the left-hand boundary again. Follow this down to the next corner, cross the stile on to a track and turn left as waymarked.

Take the next stile on your right, shortly after, into a field and follow the boundary to reach another stile. Cross this and a bridge to reach a tarmac lane, where you should turn left and then immediately right, passing over another stile into another field. Bear gently left, to drop down to reach a wide farm track. Turn left and follow this through a large metal gate, walking downhill

Arthur's Stone

and crossing a cattle grid to continue through Llan Farm. Once past this, the track becomes a tarmac lane. After a short distance, there is a grass track down to a gate on your right. Ignore this track, but take the next waymarked path on your right, diagonally downhill through a field to a stile in the hedge. Cross this and drop down some steps to reach a track. Continue over this and go through a small metal gate.

Cross through a field, which may be sown with crops, by bearing gently left to a small wooden bridge. Go over this and then a wide track to reach another small metal gate. Pass through this and continue over a slightly bigger bridge to enter some playing fields. Bear left across this towards some telegraph poles with netting to catch any wayward balls. As you reach this boundary you will see the waymark pointing in the direction to continue along this boundary fence. Pass the bowling green on the right to reach a kissing gate.

Go through the kissing gate and bear right, crossing the B4348 with care, to take the path on the other side signed to the village centre, with the church on your left. Continue on to a tarmac lane, cross over the stream, and pass the telephone box on your left. At the junction continue ahead, with the village green on your right, to reach a junction with another road. Turn left and follow this, with the Pandy Inn on your right, and, shortly after, the post office on the left. Follow the lane around to the left and take the next lane on the left, signed to Hereford and Peterchurch. This drops gently, passing Chapel Lane on your left, and continues to reach a junction with the B4348 again.

Take care here. Turn right to follow this lane, over the River Dore, to pass Lower Crossway Farm on your right. Where the B road turns sharp right, continue ahead on to a signed path (not the narrow lane), which uses the track up to a farm. Continue to climb past a property on your left and then your right and go over a cattle grid. The track then enters a field and climbs up the right-hand boundary, through a large metal gate with a stile on the left, and continues climbing through the next field.

Before the track turns right into another field, bear left to continue along the boundary on your right to reach a stile in the hedge. Cross over and then climb uphill to reach a stile by a metal gate. Cross this and follow the track uphill to the next stile and gate. As you climb over this stile, the next one becomes visible on the horizon. Head towards this stile and cross over to enter the final field with the next stile opposite. Arthur's Stone is just visible through it. After crossing this final stile, the car park is on the right.

POINTS OF INTEREST

▪ *The Pandy Inn in Dorstone dates back to around 1185, and Oliver Cromwell is known to have rested here during the Civil War.*

- *The Neolithic burial chamber known as Arthur's Stone is Herefordshire's oldest man-made structure.*
- *Images of the Golden Valley and Wye Valley inspired ideas for the Narnia books by C.S. Lewis.*

OTHER WALKS IN THE AREA

The Herefordshire Trail travels up through the Golden Valley, providing several opportunities to explore the area. Another short circular walk goes by way of Pitt Road from Dorstone up to West Lawn Common, from where paths can be taken round to Snodhill with its castle remains. Another alternative from Arthur's Stone is to drop down into the Wye Valley to Bredwardine and then return via the road up Dorstone Hill.

Hay Bluff is the nearest peak to the border book town of Hay-on-Wye, yet from the main car park it is tantalisingly obscured by its smaller foothills. A narrow lane leads up from the town to a couple of car parks near the foot of the final ascent, but if you want to appreciate the beauty of the Wye Valley to the full it is worth starting from the town itself. The views from the summit extend across Herefordshire, the Brecon Beacons and what seems like most of mid-Wales, but for a truly magical experience try tackling it in the early hours of the morning, when the mists linger. Break above the mist collecting in the Wye Valley and you will witness a sea of mist punctured by islands of hilltops.

This walk uses Offa's Dyke to leave the town and head up the foothills, which can be steep in places, before entering the Open Access area of Hay Bluff. The route stays along Offa's Dyke as it climbs the eastern flank of Hay Bluff, offering views across Herefordshire's Golden Valley, before doubling back to the summit and then dropping steeply down, following quiet country lanes and footpaths back into town.

Walk category: invigorating | Length: about 15.5km (9½ miles) | Map: Explorer Sheet OL13, Brecon Beacons National Park, Eastern Area | Parking and starting point: main car park next to craft centre in Hay-on-Wye; grid ref: SO 229 422 | Public transport: Stagecoach service 39 (Hereford–Brecon), Monday to Saturday (tel: 01633 485118) | Toilets: in craft centre complex next to car park | Nearest tourist information: Hay-on-Wye

From the main car park head back up to Oxford Road and turn right away from the craft centre. Shortly after passing a doctor's

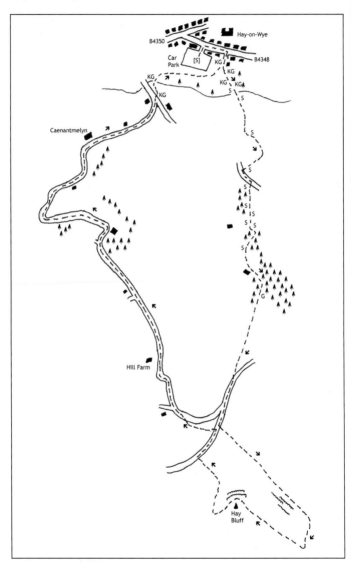

Map 31: Hay Bluff

surgery on your right, take the track on your right, signed as Offa's Dyke, that weaves between two buildings. At the end of the track pass through a kissing gate to enter a field. Cross this, following the left-hand boundary, ignore a stile on your left and continue to the end of the field. Pass through another kissing gate and cross the next field, this time along the right-hand edge. Continue through a third kissing gate and across another field. Enter the next field through yet another kissing gate and stay along the left-hand boundary to reach a stiled bridge. Cross this and climb up to a stile.

Go over this stile and continue into the next field, keeping to the left-hand edge to reach another stile. Cross this and continue along a fenced boundary to enter the next field. Head straight across to the stile opposite, which is next to a large metal gate. Cross over this and a farm track, and bear gently left towards a telegraph pole. As you approach this, bear to the right of this and follow the field edge around to your right as waymarked. At the end of this field, cross over a stile and drop down on to a lane. Turn left, to climb gently.

Take the next Offa's Dyke signed path on your right, over a stile into a field and along the right-hand boundary. Turn right, as signed, over a wooden bridge and then a stile, turning left into the next field. Climb up to another stile, cross this and a small wooden footbridge, this time continuing up along the boundary on your right. The path passes through into another field along this edge to reach a stile. Cross over this and a track, then climb up a few steps to another stile. Cross over and climb up through this field. This is the steepest section so far. The path bears right through some trees and then left into another field. Continue up to another stile and then on to a track. Turn left.

Follow this track for a brief respite along the level, passing a cottage on the right and continuing, as signed, into the trees, where the path appears to fork. Bear left, go over a stream and walk alongside a woodland boundary on your left. The path then drops down to a wider path to reach a large wooden gate. Go

Lord Hereford's Knob as seen from Hay Bluff

through this and head upwards on to the open hillside, where you catch your first proper sight of Hay Bluff.

Follow the path around to the right, passing the remains of a small quarried area on your right, and look out for some large stones with the national trail acorn symbols and directional arrows painted in them. Follow this path, as signed, heading towards Hay Bluff across the open hillside. After the third marker stone the route drops down through a ditch, with another marker stone, before climbing back out and heading up towards a tarmac lane.

At the fifth stone marker bear right on to the lane and follow this uphill. Ignore a lane on your right, but shortly after turn left to continue along Offa's Dyke and on to designated Open Access land. Follow the path through the bracken, dropping down to a

ditch and then bearing right to stay on Offa's Dyke. Begin to climb again, following the path across another ditch and climbing up on to a wide, grassy path that begins a long, slow climb up the eastern side of Hay Bluff. This climbs steadily, passing another Offa's Dyke marker, with good views to your left of the Golden Valley. Welcome back into England, by the way, as the path crosses the border.

Eventually, the path bears right on to a stone path, which then becomes a flag-stoned route across a boggy area, where it levels out. At a junction with another stone path, turn right and follow this, back into Wales, to reach the triangulation point marking the summit of Hay Bluff. There are great views from the summit here across the Wye Valley and mid-Wales. The noticeable peak to your left is Lord Hereford's Knob.

From the trig point follow the stone path left. Shortly afterwards take the obvious path on your right, which doubles back, to drop down the northern face of Hay Bluff. This is a popular route for those climbing up from the car parks that are visible from here. The route drops quickly and then bears left down the lower slopes to reach the tarmac lane, beside a car park. At the lane, turn right and follow the lane downhill. When you reach the turning for Offa's Dyke on your right, turn left on to a grass path between bracken, dropping down beside another lane, which you need to join just before the cattle grid. Cross over this and follow the lane around to your right.

Where this lane forks, bear right and wander gently downhill, passing Hill Farm on your left and continuing between high hedges, to reach another junction. Ignore the lane on your left and continue ahead. This lane now drops steeply towards a farm. Follow it around to the left and continue downhill, ignoring the path on your right, which is signed to Hay. The lane bears around to the right once again, maintaining its downward direction and eventually passing Caenantmelyn on your left. Ignore the narrow lane on your right and continue gently downhill, passing another cottage on your left, until you reach a junction with another lane.

Turn left and bear to the right-hand side of some metal railings, walking along the verge to leave the lane and reach a kissing gate. Go through and follow the right-hand boundary edge, passing some small business workshops on the left. Follow this path round to another kissing gate on your right, go through and cross over a bridge into a field. Head to the diagonally opposite corner kissing gate, which you may recognise. Pass through this and then follow the track back up to the road into Hay-on-Wye, turning left to return to the car park.

POINTS OF INTEREST

▮ *Scenes from the 1981 film* An American Werewolf in London *were filmed on the lane just beneath Hay Bluff.*

Hay on Wye from the Castle Bookshop

- *Richard Booth helped make Hay-on-Wye the book town it is today, with nearly 40 bookstores.*
- *When the former US President Bill Clinton visited the Hay Festival in 2002 he referred to it as the 'Woodstock of the mind'.*

OTHER WALKS IN THE AREA

If you park in one of the car parks nearer to Hay Bluff you can explore the other peaks, Lord Hereford's Knob and Waun Fach in the Black Mountains during another invigorating walk. For something more relaxing follow the Wye Valley walk along the banks of this border river.

The abbey at Dore was founded in 1147 by Cistercian monks from Morimond Abbey in France. The church on the site wasn't consecrated until 1282, however, when the service was carried out by the bishop of Hereford, although the bishop of St David's claimed that the abbey fell within his jurisdiction. Today, only a little remains of what was a substantial collection of buildings, although that little is now a spectacular parish church, which is worth exploring. What was the nave area is now covered by the churchyard, and the surrounding fields would have had further buildings on them. Walk around the back of the abbey and you can still see some of the remains of the chapter house and the cloisters.

Nearby Abbey Dore Court Garden has 2.43 hectares (6 acres) of gardens, which can be explored on some days of the week in summer (visit www.abbeydorecourt.co.uk for further details). This walk allows you to explore both places as well as to take in some of the views of the valley. There is limited parking in the village, so park considerately; alternatively, a regular bus service stops at the village. This route allows you to explore the abbey grounds and then follow the River Dore with its dragonflies, birds and, now, water voles, before climbing gently up some quiet lanes to look out over the valley.

Walk category: easy | Length: about 7.75km (4¾ miles) | Map: Explorer Sheet OL13, Brecon Beacons National Park, Eastern Area | Parking and starting point: limited parking by Abbey Dore village hall; grid ref: SO 385 305 | Public transport: Nick Maddy Coaches service 440 (Michaelchurch Escley–Hereford), Monday to Saturday (tel: 01432 266211) | Toilets: none | Nearest tourist information: Hereford

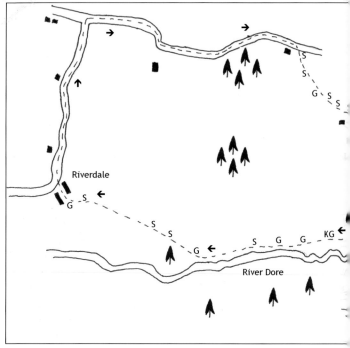

Map 32: Abbey Dore

From the village hall return to the main road. Turn left and follow the road briefly. Take care, because it can be busy. Continue until you reach the lich-gate for Dore Abbey on your left. Pass through the gate and drop down on to the tarmac path. To explore the abbey (which is highly recommended) follow the tarmac path to the main entrance. To follow this walk bear right on to a grass path, at the point where the tarmac path turns left to the main entrance. The grass path continues around the right-hand side of the abbey and heads towards a kissing gate. Before

Overleaf: River Dore

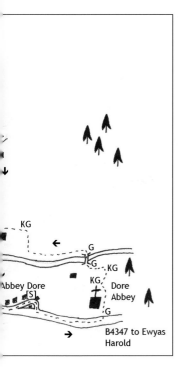

you reach this gate, however, it's worth taking the grass path on your left, which allows you to explore the remains of the cloister grounds.

Continue through the kissing gate, as waymarked, towards another kissing gate, which leads you into a field that may contain livestock. Head across this field towards a wooden kissing gate and then straight over a small wooden bridge. Bear gently left across this next field, to a wooden gate on the opposite side. Go through this, straight on to a concrete bridge over the River Dore, and then through another wooden gate, before following the path around to the left as it follows the river.

After a short distance the path turns sharp right to follow the perimeter of Abbey Dore Court Gardens. It then turns sharp left. Go through another kissing gate to the left of a large metal gate and continue ahead until you pick up a wide track that eventually leads to a lane. Turn left and follow this, passing the entrance to Abbey Dore Court Gardens on your left. Ignore this for the time being, and continue along the lane, but before this crosses the river take the next footpath signed on your right. Cross over a stile and shortly afterwards go through a wooden gate and follow the path, which is waymarked as the Herefordshire Trail. This path runs between two fences, with the River Dore audible to your left and crop

Dore Abbey

fields on your right. Pass through another kissing gate to enter a crop field and follow the left-hand field boundary.

Continue through a large metal gate. The path now draws closer to the river on your left. At the end of the field go through a large metal gate and then bear left through a hedge line, over a stile as waymarked, to continue along the riverbank. The path follows this for a short while, with a fence on your right-hand side. Just before a fence blocks off the route along the riverside ahead, bear right through a large metal gate to enter a field, which may contain livestock. Head towards the stile in the fence, cross this to enter a crop field and continue across this to another stile in the opposite fence.

Cross over this stile, as waymarked, and bear right through this field, which is used for animal grazing, heading towards another stile in the hedge, to the left of a large metal gate. Cross over this and follow the hedge line on your right to enter a garden area. Turn left, as signed, around the garden, and then turn right, to follow a grass path up through a large wooden gate to a waymark post and then on to a tarmac lane between properties, marked on the OS map as Riverdale, until you reach a quiet lane. Turn right and follow this lane uphill.

The lane ambles gently uphill, passing properties on both sides, but there are soon some good views to be had behind you of the Golden Valley and the Black Mountains in the distance. Follow this lane until you reach a junction with another lane, where you can see a notice board for Abbey Dore and Bacton parish council under the signpost. Turn right here and follow this gently uphill.

The lane soon levels out, offering good views to your right over the valley once more. Follow the lane as it bears gently right, passing the entrance to Longwood on the right, before turning sharp right, then left. After a short distance the lane drops steeply through some trees and then levels once again, before climbing to pass a property on the right. Take the next signed footpath on the right, cross over the stile and head straight across the field to the stile opposite. Cross this to enter another field with good views to the right. Head towards the metal gate opposite, and in the distance you will see the unusually shaped hill of Skirrid Fawr. It looks as if the middle has been scooped out of it, although it is an optical illusion – it's actually two hills.

Go through the metal gate and head across this field, dropping down to find a stile in the hedge. Cross over this and turn left, as signed, to drop down steeply through the undergrowth, eventually emerging on an open hillside. Continue to head downhill, along the left-hand boundary edge, to reach another stile. Cross this and cut downhill, trying to keep to the left-hand boundary, to reach a stile in the bottom corner. Climb over this and then drop down a couple of wooden steps to reach a farm track. Turn left and follow this to reach a tarmac lane.

Turn right on to this lane and follow it gently downhill. Ignore the lane on your left and continue downwards, passing a few properties on both sides of the road and eventually reaching the entrance to Abbey Dore Court Gardens once more. If the gardens are open, it is worth stopping off now to explore them.

The walk continues along the lane, crossing over the River Dore before gently climbing up to reach the junction with the B4347. Turn left here to pass the bus stop and return to the village hall.

POINTS OF INTEREST

- *Did a misunderstanding by a French monk give the Golden Valley its name? The river that runs through the valley is the River Dore, which takes its name from the welsh dwr, which means 'water'. However, when pronounced, dwr sounds like the French d'or, which means 'of gold'.*
- *Dore Abbey is the only Cistercian abbey in Britain to be founded from the Morimond Abbey in France. The remains of the Cistercian abbey were 'restored' in 1632–4 by Viscount Scudamore, who removed the nave and aisles and made the presbytery and ambulatory into the parish church.*
- *The cottages marked as Riverdale on the map used to be the workhouse for Abbey Dore.*
- *Look out for water voles, which have been recently re-introduced in this area.*

OTHER WALKS IN THE AREA

Both the Herefordshire Trail and Marches Way pass through this section of the Golden Valley.

WALK 33 | Mordiford

The River Wye becomes more relaxed after it has passed through Hereford, and where one of its tributaries, the River Lugg joins it, buzzards may be seen soaring overhead, swans swim majestically, and herons patrol the waters. It's a typical English scene and a popular place for local anglers, who come to wile away hot, sunny afternoons. During the years when he lived in Hereford, the composer Sir Edward Elgar enjoyed cycling down to Mordiford Bridge to do a spot of fishing.

This lollipop-shaped walk begins from the picnic site at Swardon Quarry, which provides a great viewpoint across the floodplain of the River Wye towards Hereford. The views continue at the beginning of the walk, but it then drops down into Mordiford to cross the bridge over the River Lugg, following this tributary until it meets the River Wye. This relatively level section follows the Wye round to Hampton Bishop by way of the Wye Valley Walk, before passing through Hampton Bishop, to pick up the River Lugg once more to return to Mordiford, retracing your steps to Swardon Quarry. It's pleasant at any time of year but best in summer.

Walk category: moderate | Length: about 12.5km (7¾ miles) | Map: Explorer Sheet 189, Hereford and Ross-on-Wye | Parking and starting point: Swardon Quarry picnic site, near Prior's Frome; grid ref: SO 577 385 | Public transport: First Bus service 453/454 (Hereford–Woolhope) stops at Hampton Bishop and Mordiford, Monday to Saturday (tel: 01905 359393) | Toilets: none | Nearest tourist information: Hereford

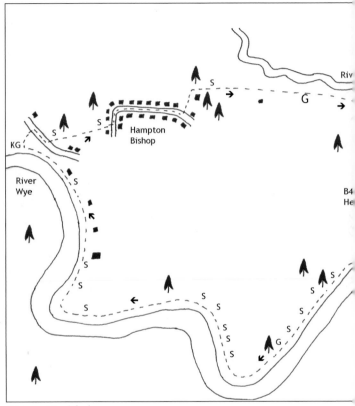

Map 33: Mordiford

With your back to the viewpoint, leave the car park to pick up the
lane and bear right. Ignoring the signed bridleway on the right,
take the next track on the right, turning left immediately after on
to a footpath that is signed as the Mordiford Loop. Climb up
through the trees, before taking the next path on your right,
signed to Checkley Barn picnic site. Cross over the stile and
follow the grass path between two fences. There are good views
across to Hereford on your right.

Minor road to
Prior's Frome

[S]

Car
Park

S

S

S

S

S

S

†

Mordiford

River Wye

At the next stile, to the left of a metal gate, cross over and continue over a crossing track to stay on the wide path between two fields. Follow this between gateposts to climb up to another stile to the right of a metal gate. Cross over this and enter a field. Follow the right-hand boundary, as signed, and then go through a gap in the hedge to enter the next field. The path now follows the left-hand boundary, gently dropping and bearing right to a stile. Cross this to enter the trees and continue dropping, steeply in places, to reach a wide track. Turn right and follow this downhill, passing properties on your left, to reach a tarmac lane. Turn right here and use the pedestrian path.

Follow this to the next road junction in Mordiford, with the Moon Inn on your right. Turn right but cross over to the other side of the road when you can to pick up the pedestrian path through Mordiford, continuing past the post office on your left. Eventually, the pedestrian path runs out, just as you reach Mordiford Bridge. Take care as you cross over this long bridge, which is not wide enough for two cars.

At the end of the bridge take the next signed footpath on your left to climb away from the road and then drop down steps to a

River Wye and Haugh Wood

stile. Cross this to enter a field, following the bank of the River Lugg on your left. The river gently bears round to the right, and the path continues to a stiled wooden bridge on the left, which leads into the next field. Cross this and remain along the banks of the Lugg, with the earth flood defence visible on your right. You will soon reach the corner of the field, where the Lugg flows into the River Wye. Turn right to continue along the riverbank, but now following the Wye.

At the next field edge cross the stile and continue ahead. Just before you reach the next tree line, bear gently away from the

river to take the stile in the trees just to the left of a track on top of the flood defences. Once you are in the next field, bear left, back towards the riverbank, to follow the path. Go through the next field boundary, using the stiled wooden bridge, and continue along the river, noticing that the flood defence has veered away to your right. The path goes through into the next field by way of a stiled bridge and follows the river round to the next boundary, reaching a large metal gate.

Go through the gate to pick up a wide track alongside the river. Watch out for birds nesting in the cliffs on the other side of the

Herefordshire from Swarden Quarry viewpoint

Wye. The river veers sharp right, and the path leads up to a stile to the left of a gate. Cross over to continue, passing under some power cables, and then cross over two more stiles to enter the next field. Follow this round to the next stile, and cross this to enter the next field, wandering under some more power lines, to reach a stile to the left of a metal gate. Cross over and continue along the riverbank. During the summer months this section of river is busy with swans gliding up- and downstream.

Cross over the next stile to follow the river, before it turns sharp right again, following the path as waymarked along the

water's edge and not on the track higher up. It can get quite tight walking among the trees here, but soon the path reaches a stile. Cross over and climb up to rejoin the earth flood defences, which join from the right. Then bear left over a stile beside a wooden gate. Follow the grass path along the top of the flood defences, continuing over another stile beside a gate. The path passes the Bunch of Carrots public house on your right and then bears left, and soon the Wye turns sharply left away from you.

Continue ahead to reach a kissing gate. Go through the gate and turn right, dropping down some steps to reach the B4224.

Turn right here. Take care, because there is no footpath, and cross over to the other side when you see the lay-by opposite.

Pass by the telephone box and bus stop, then turn left on to a signed footpath. Cross over a stile to enter a field and head across this, picking up a boundary fence on your right when you are halfway across. Cross over the next stile and continue between two properties to reach a lane. Turn left and follow the lane through Hampton Bishop. Ignore the signed footpath on your left and continue, passing a thatched cottage on your left. Ignore two more paths on your left and right, and follow the lane past another thatched cottage, this time on the right. Where the lane turns right, take the signed footpath on your left, following a track up between some properties. Turn right, as waymarked, to follow a tight path between some fir trees and a fence. Cross over a stile to join a wide track.

Follow this track between fields and, ignoring the stile on your left, continue ahead, as waymarked, on the permissive path. You will notice that this track travels along the top of another flood defence. Continue under some power lines and then go through a large gate to enter an unfenced area. The path continues along the top of this flood defence, with the River Lugg away to your left, all the way back round to Mordiford Bridge. Just before you reach the bridge, turn right to drop down to a stile, cross over and follow the path between fencing to reach a stile by the road. Cross this and then turn left to cross over the bridge, once more taking care.

To return to your car follow the same route back. Continue through Mordiford village and take the lane on your left, after the Moon Inn. Follow the tarmac path and, where this stops, turn left, as signed, uphill. Just before you reach the large gate, turn left, as signed, to follow the path up through the trees, eventually reaching a stile. Cross over and follow the right-hand field boundary, uphill and round to the left, to pass into the next field. Follow its left-hand boundary and cross over the stile by the gate to pick up the grass path, which drops gently, over a crossing track, and then over a stile to climb gently on a grass track. Cross over the stile to enter the trees again and turn left, dropping back down to the road by the car park.

POINTS OF INTEREST

- *Mordiford Bridge is where many of Edward Elgar's sketches for his ode* The Music Makers, *composed in 1911–12 as a setting of the poem by A. O'Shaughnessy, were made.*
- *In July 2005 a pair of bee-eaters, whose usual home is southern Europe, nested in the mud banks of the River Wye near Hampton Bishop.*
- *Sections of Mordiford Bridge are believed to date back to 1352.*

OTHER WALKS IN THE AREA

This walk can be shortened to an 8km (5 mile) circular route, which might interest those using public transport. Car drivers can park in the lay-by at Hampton Bishop by the Bunch of Carrots public house, which is where the bus stops. Follow the route round to Mordiford Bridge, then cross over the road and follow the Lugg to where it joins the Wye and then back round to Hampton Bishop. The full Mordiford Loop, sections of which are included on this walk, is a gentle 6.4km (4 mile) circular route, exploring the countryside to the east of Mordiford.

WALK 34 | Sugar Loaf

At a height of 596m (1,955ft), the Sugar Loaf doesn't quite make it into the Welsh mountain league table, but the views from this pinnacle are certainly worth the effort. If you look north it's possible to see the Black Mountains towards Hay-on-Wye, and there are the Usk Valley to the west, the large mound of Blorenge to the south and Monmouthshire to the southeast. Despite the height, the peak isn't visible from the centre of Abergavenny, so it's not until you climb out of the town that you catch your first real glimpse. The final ascent is the steepest, making a rest at the summit plateau the perfect excuse to soak up the views.

This walk begins from the main car park in Abergavenny, although the railway station isn't far away. It meanders through the residential streets and then climbs up Y Deri, one of the Sugar Loaf's foothills, and follows this ridge around the Parc Lodge Estate, before the final ascent to the top. The return journey follows the Rholben Ridge, from where there are great views over the town, before dropping back into its outskirts.

Walk category: invigorating | Length: about 12km (7½ miles) | Map: Explorer Sheet OL13, Brecon Beacons National Park, Eastern Area | Parking and starting point: Fairfield car park in the centre of Abergavenny; grid ref: SO 300 145 | Public transport: several services run through Abergavenny, including Stagecoach service X4 (Hereford–Cardiff), Monday to Saturday (tel: 01633 485118); Abergavenny is also on the Manchester–Cardiff rail line | Toilets: White Horse Lane, Abergavenny town centre | Nearest tourist information: Abergavenny

Sugar Loaf as seen from Y Deri

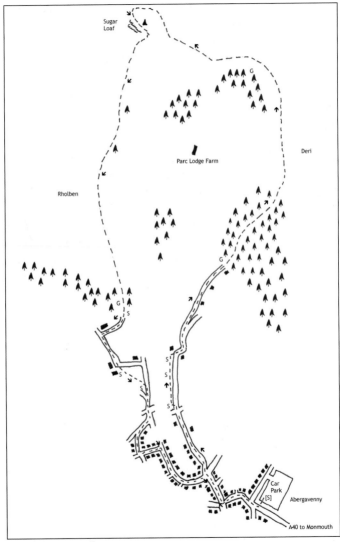

Map 34: Sugar Loaf

From the Fairfield car park head towards the pedestrian crossing that takes you to the shops, but don't use it. Instead, turn right along Park Road and follow this around to the left, towards another pedestrian crossing near Tesco on the left. Before you reach this, bear right into Pen-Y-Pound, passing a church on your right and another on your left and yet another on your left further up. Cross over the road by the primary school and at a traffic light-controlled junction continue straight over, on to a road that is still called Pen-Y-Pound. Pass a football ground on the right and later a school, after which the road begins to climb. Go past an education and conference centre on the right, where you lose the pedestrian path, and climb up along the narrow road until you reach a crossroads.

Bear left, to take a signed footpath between the road on your left and the one ahead, crossing over a stile and into a field. Follow the right-hand field boundary and climb up, passing under power lines to reach another stile. Cross this and continue through the next field along this edge to the end, go over the next stile and continue climbing on a tarmac lane between cottages.

The lane turns sharp right, climbs, and then bears around to the left, continuing between trees. Soon the lane appears to fork. Bear left to continue along the side of a valley, where you will get your first good glimpse of Sugar Loaf on the left. The lane levels and travels along the valley, before eventually reaching a large wooden gate near a property on the right. Go through this gate to enter the National Trust land of Y Deri. Climb up the main footpath, ignoring any side tracks as you wander up between these old trees, including any larger paths that bear off to the left. Continue to climb up until you break through the other side of the wood on to open, bracken-covered hillside. Go straight over a grass crossing track and climb up, maintaining the same direction, to reach a stone wall.

Bear left here, around the corner of the stone wall, heading towards Sugar Loaf on a grass path and with the wall on your left.

View from Sugar Loaf

At times the wall disappears and is replaced by wire fencing, but the path is relatively level. At a junction with another track, continue ahead, with Sugar Loaf on your left and Skirrid Fawr around to your right. Where this grass path forks, bear left up towards a hillock, climb over and drop down the other side to reach a junction with another track. Turn left here, towards what now looks like an imposing Sugar Loaf.

Ignore a large wooden gate, which would take you into the National Trust's Parc Lodge, and continue along the path that skirts around the grounds and the head of the valley. At a fork, just as the path begins to climb, bear right to climb up through the bracken. The climb begins to get steeper, and you will eventually be clambering up a short, near-vertical section, after which it then bears right to reach a wide crossing track. Continue straight over on to a smaller path, which still climbs but which

takes a long, circuitous route around the right-hand side of Sugar Loaf.

Follow this around the northern edge of the hill. Go straight over a wide crossing track and continue around to the left, where the path becomes rockier on its final ascent to the summit, just in front of the triangulation point. Have a rest and a bite to eat while you enjoy the views, but be careful because the sheep here are aware that many rucksacks contain food.

To begin the descent, head along the summit plateau towards Abergavenny and then bear right down a small track. Ignore a zigzagging stone path off to the right but continue ahead, dropping down towards a grass path that can be seen running along the right-hand side of a small brook. The path drops steeply down to this ditch and then runs parallel to it, eventually dropping down to cross over the stream and climb up the other side, continuing through the bracken. Go straight over a crossing track and, shortly after, fork left to reach a junction. Bear right on to a track, which soon has a boundary fence running along your left-hand side.

Continue along here, dropping gently for about 1.6km (1 mile), with the route you used to climb Sugar Loaf visible on the other side of the valley on your left. Where the fence turns sharp left, continue ahead on the grass path and then begin dropping sharply. There are some good views of Abergavenny in front of you. Go over a small crossing track and drop down to a small metal gate. Go through this and drop down through the undergrowth to reach a wide track. Turn right and follow this down to a stile on the right of a large gate. Cross this and follow the track downhill to reach a junction with a tarmac lane.

Turn left and follow this down towards some properties. Where the lane turns sharp left, continue ahead on to a signed footpath, crossing a stile on the left of a gate. Enter the field and bear gently left along a path, which passes a lone fir tree before it picks up a boundary fence on the right. Drop down closer to the fence and, shortly after this, cross over a stile. Continue along this path with the fence on your right and a sunken lane on your left.

Where the path joins the lane at a crossroads, continue ahead, downhill, passing Pentre Lane on your right and, shortly after, Pentre Road on your right. Continue into Chapel Road and follow this into a residential area to some crossroads. Turn left into Linden Avenue. At the other end turn right into Avenue Road. Ignore all other side roads and follow Avenue Road round to your left to reach the traffic light-controlled junction at Pen-Y-Pound once again. Turn right to pass all three churches again, and at the bottom of this road bear left to follow the main road, back around to the car park.

POINTS OF INTEREST

▪ *When Rudolph Hess was captured in Scotland during the Second World War, he was actually held prisoner in Abergavenny. He could*

*often be seen, accompanied by prison guards, walking up to the summit
of Sugar Loaf.*

■ *Another smaller hill in Wales, also called Sugar Loaf, can be found
between Llanwrtyd Wells and Cynghordy, and it even has its own
station – the most remote station on the Heart of Wales Railway Line.*

■ *Seven grape varieties are grown on the Sugar Loaf Vineyard,
producing award-winning wines.*

OTHER WALKS IN THE AREA

To the south of the town is Blorenge, with the Punchbowl nature
reserve, while to the east is Skirrid Fawr, both of which are worth
climbing. For something a little gentler there are several paths
exploring the banks of the River Usk from the town.

WALK 35 | Symonds Yat

The horseshoe loop caused as the River Wye negotiates its final journey towards Chepstow is some 8km (5 miles) long, and the view from the 152.4m (500ft) high outcrop stretches eastwards into England. The viewpoint at Yat Rock is popular with bird-watchers, who come to view the peregrine falcons nesting on Coldwell Rocks.

This walk begins near the viewpoint, giving you an opportunity to survey most of the first section of this route, which drops down to the eastern side of the loop and follows the River Wye round to the bottom of Huntsman Hill, where the path cuts left to pick up the western side of the loop further downstream. Here, small ferries operate to whisk you to the other side of the river, where inns await to serve you if the inns on this side of the river don't tempt you beforehand. The route continues along the river before diverting back uphill through Mailscot Wood.

Walk category: moderate | Length: about 10.5km (6½ miles) | Map: Explorer Sheet OL14, Wye Valley and the Forest of Dean | Parking and starting point: main car park at Symonds Yat on B4432; grid ref: SO 563 157 | Public transport: Dukes Travel service 709 (Coleford–Symonds Yat), Tuesday and Friday only (tel: 01594 835476) | Toilets: at car park and near Saracens Head public house, Symonds Yat East | Nearest tourist information: Ross-on-Wye

From the car park head towards the toilets and then bear right on to a wide track, which is signed towards the viewpoints and refresh-

River Wye

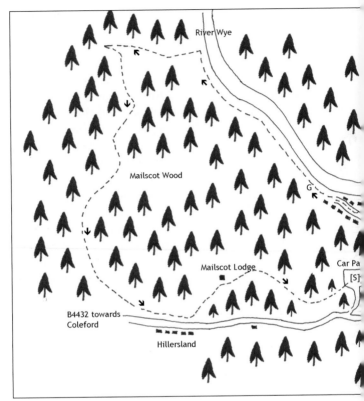

Map 35: Symonds Yat

ments. At a junction turn left, as signed, to continue to the viewpoints, passing the refreshment cabin on your left. The are several vantage points from this section, all worth exploring, but to continue the walk turn right over the footbridge and then turn left. This takes you to another viewpoint with a toposcope, and this is the best place to see the peregrine falcons nesting on Coldwell Rocks.

When you are ready to continue, return to the footbridge, but don't cross it. Instead, continue ahead towards the road. Turn sharp

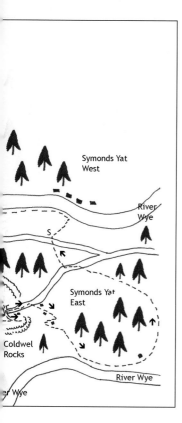

right on to the road, under the footbridge, and continue to drop downhill. Take care, because this narrow road is used by cars. Turn right, just before Cliffe Cottage, on to a footpath signed to Welsh Bicknor. This path bears right away from the cottage and zigzags downhill, behind Wren Cottage, into the trees. At the next waymarked junction, turn left to continue dropping towards the river. Climb down a set of large wooden steps, then turn left on to a wide track, before turning right, where signed, down some stone steps. This path continues around a stone ruin before bearing right, as signed, eventually opening up on to a grass path by the riverside.

Follow this path along the Wye, passing an idyllic cottage on your left, before veering left between fences and hedges and around some large rocky outcrops. Climb some steps and, at a junction, bear left uphill on more steps. The path continues upwards, passing another stone ruin on your left. When the path levels out turn left, as signed, up some more steps.

Turn right on to a large, wide track and follow this as it gently bends around to the left and descends. Where the bend to the left sharpens, turn left, as signed, on to a smaller path. This drops down to a single-track lane with passing places. Bear left to climb

Ye Oldie Ferrie Inne

up, but look out for the signed footpath on your right. Take this as it continues to descend towards another lane. Bear left on to this lane and, almost immediately, turn right, across a stile, heading across a field.

Thirsty walkers can try to summon the ferry to take them to Ye Olde Ferrie Inne on the other side of the River Wye for some refreshment. To continue the walk, however, turn left and follow the riverbank. At the end of this field continue through into the grounds of the canoe centre, along the riverbank, bearing left where signed, through the centre's entrance, on to a small road. Turn right along here, passing some toilets on your right, followed shortly by the Saracen's Head public house on your left.

Continue along the road, passing the Forest View Hotel and up the approach to the Royal Hotel. Bear right into the car park and continue along the paving slabs to reach a metal barrier gate. Go around this to pick up the wide forest track. Follow this track and, where it forks, bear right to use a path that follows the riverbank.

The path later bears left to rejoin the track, but immediately afterwards bear right to return to the riverbank. This wide, grass path follows the river for some distance, before eventually bearing left to rejoin a track that may be used by cyclists. Turn right to continue following the river downstream.

At a waymarked junction ignore the turning on your left and continue ahead along the river. When you reach a junction where this track meets some larger forestry tracks turn left on to a wide track, which meanders uphill into the woods. Continue along here, but keep watch for a signed footpath on your right. When you see it, don't take it. Instead, take the footpath on your left, which doubles back slightly, before climbing up on a stony path.

Where this path forks, bear left and enjoy the meandering route through the broadleaved trees. At the next junction continue ahead, as signed, following this path as it begins to climb. Bear left where the path forks to continue on the level, and at the next junction continue straight over on to a smaller track, which then drops down. At the next junction turn right on to a wide forest track, which gently climbs once more.

Where this track forks bear left to remain on the wider track and then ignore the next wide track on your left. Continue to climb as the track gently bears around to the left. Ignore another large track, this time on your right, and continue to climb as this track bears further round to the left. The path then goes under some power lines to reach another junction of paths near some houses. Turn left on to the smaller path, which goes back under the power lines. Cross straight over a wide track and follow the path as it passes around a property on your left.

The path begins to drop downhill once again, and at a junction with a wide forest track you should turn right. When you reach a tarmac lane, cross straight over with care, and continue ahead, ignoring any side tracks. At the next tarmac lane, turn left to follow this back into the car park.

River Wye and Coldwell Rocks

POINTS OF INTEREST

- *Yat is a local term for gate or pass.*
- *The best time of year to view the peregrine falcons is between April and August, when the RSPB sets up viewing telescopes.*
- *At nearby King Arthur's Cave archaeological finds have included the remains of bears and sabre-toothed tigers.*

OTHER WALKS IN THE AREA

From Symonds Yat follow the road to join the B4229 round to Goodrich, cross over the Wye and follow the Wye Valley Walk back. Alternatively, there are numerous other tracks and paths through the Wye Valley Woods, which are owned by the Forestry Commission.

APPENDIX 1 | Tourist Information Centre Contact Details

Abergavenny
Swan Meadow, Monmouth Road, Abergavenny NP7 5HH
Tel: 01873 857588; Email: abergavenny.tic@monmouthshire.gov.uk

Bridgnorth
The Library, Listley Street, Bridgnorth WV16 4AW
Tel: 01746 763257; Email: Bridgnorth.tourism@shropshire-cc.gov.uk

Builth Wells
The Groe Car Park, Builth Wells, Powys LD2 3BT
Tel: 01982 553307; Email: builtic@powys.gov.uk

Church Stretton
Church Street, Church Stretton SY6 6DG
Tel: 01694 723133; Email: churchstretton.tourism@shropshire-cc.gov.uk

Elan Valley Visitor Centre (seasonal opening)
Elan Valley, Rhayader, Powys LD6 5HP
Tel: 01597 810898; Email: info@elanvalley.org.uk

Ellesmere the Mereside
Ellesmere, Shropshire SY12 0HD
Tel: 01691 622981; Email: ellesmere.tourism@shropshire-cc.gov.uk

Hay-on-Wye
Craft Centre, Hay-on-Wye HR3 5AE
Tel: 01497 820144

Hereford
1 King Street, Hereford HR4 9BW
Tel: 01432 268430; Email: tic-hereford@herefordshire.gov.uk

Ironbridge
The Tollhouse, Ironbridge, Telford TF8 7JS
Tel: 01952 884391; Email: tic@ironbridge.org.uk

Kington
2 Mill Street, Kington, Herefordshire HR5 3BQ
Tel: 01544 230778; Email: contact@kingtontourist.fsnet.co.uk

Knighton
Offa's Dyke Centre, West Street, Knighton, Powys LD7 1EN
Tel: 01547 529424; Email: oda@offasdyke.demon.co.uk

Lake Vyrnwy
Unit 2, Vyrnwy Craft Workshops, Lake Vyrnwy, Powys SY10 0LY
Tel: 01691 870346; Email: lactic@powys.gov.uk

Leominster
1 Corn Square, Leominster, Herefordshire HR6 8LR
Tel: 01568 616460; Email: tic-leominster@herefordshire.gov.uk

Llandrindod Wells
The Old Town Hall, Memorial Gardens, Llandrindod Wells,
Powys LD1 5DL
Tel: 01597 822600; Email: llandtic@powys.gov.uk

Llangollen
Y Chapel, Castle Street, Llangollen, Denbighshire LL20 8NU
Tel: 01978 860828; Email: Llangollen@nwtic.com

Loggerheads Country Park
nr Mold, Denbighshire CH7 5LH
Tel: 01352 810586

Ludlow
Castle Street, Ludlow, Shropshire SY8 1AS
Tel: 01584 875053; Email: ludlow.tourism@shropshire-cc.gov.uk

Much Wenlock
The Museum, High Street, Much Wenlock, Shropshire TF13 6HR
Tel: 01952 727679; Email: muchwenlock.tourism@shropshire-cc.gov.uk

Newtown
The Park, Back Lane, Newtown, Powys SY216 2PW
Tel: 01686 625580; Email: newtic@powys.gov.uk

Queenswood
Queenswood Country Park, Dinmore Hill, Leominster,
Herefordshire HR6 0PY
Tel: 01568 797842; Email: queenswoodtic@herefordshire.gov.uk

Rhayader
The Leisure Centre, Rhayader, Powys LD6 5BY
Tel: 01597 810591; Email: Rhayader.tic@powys.gov.uk

Ross-on-Wye
Swan House, Edde Cross Street, Ross-on-Wye, Herefordshire HR9 7BZ
Tel: 01989 562768; Email: tic-ross@herefordshire.gov.uk

Shrewsbury
The Music Hall, The Square, Shrewsbury SY1 1LH
Tel: 01743 281200; Email: visitorinfo@shrewsbury.gov.uk

Telford
The Telford Shopping Centre, Telford TF3 4BX
Tel: 01952 230032
Email: tourist-info@telfordshopping.co.uk

Welshpool
Vicarage Gardens, Welshpool, Powys SY21 7DD
Tel: 01938 552043; Email: weltic@powys.gov.uk

Wrexham
Lambpit Street, Wrexham LL11 1AY
Tel: 01978 292015; Email: tic@wrexham.gov.uk

APPENDIX 2 | Useful Contacts

CADW (Historic Monuments and Properties)
Cadw, Welsh Assembly Government, Plas Carew, Unit 5/7, Cefn Coed,
Parc Nantgarw, Cardiff CF15 7QQ
Tel: 01443 33 6000; Web: www.cadw.wales.gov.uk

Countryside Access (England)
Web: www.countrysideaccess.gov.uk

Countryside Access (Wales)
Web: www.ccw.gov.uk

English Heritage
Customer Services, PO Box 569, Swindon SN2 2YP
Tel: 0870 333 1181; Web: www.english-heritage.org.uk

Forestry Commission
Web: www.forestry.gov.uk

Heart of Wales Railway Line
Web: www.heart-of-wales.co.uk

National Trust
Web: www.nationaltrust.org.uk

National Trust West Midlands (includes Shropshire and Herefordshire)
Attingham Park, Shrewsbury, Shropshire SY4 4TP
Tel: 01743 708100

National Trust North West (includes Cheshire)
18 Market Street, Altrincham, Cheshire WA14 1PH
Tel: 0161 928 0075

National Trust Wessex (includes Gloucestershire)
Eastleigh Court, Bishopstrow, Warminster, Wiltshire BA12 9HW
Tel: 01985 843600

National Trust Wales
Trinity Square, Llandudno, Conwy LL30 2DE
Tel: 01492 860123

Offa's Dyke Association
The Offa's Dyke Centre, Knighton, Powys LD7 1EN
Tel: 01547 528753; Web: www.offasdyke.demon.co.uk

Ordnance Survey
Customer Service Centre, Ordnance Survey, Romsey Road,
Southampton SO16 4GU
Tel: 08456 050505; Web: www.ordnancesurvey.co.uk

Ramblers Association (National/England)
2nd Floor, Camelford House, 87–90 Albert Embankment,
London SE1 7TW
Tel: 020 7339 8500; Web: www.ramblers.org.uk

Ramblers Association (Wales)
3 Coopers Yard, Curran Road, Cardiff CF10 5NB
Tel: 029 2064 4308; Web: www.ramblers.org.uk/wales

Traveline (Wales)
Tel: 0870 608 2 608
Web: www.traveline-cymru.org.uk

Traveline (West Midlands)
Tel: 0870 608 2 608; Web: www.travelinemidlands.co.uk

Wildlife Trusts
Brecknock Wildlife Trust
Lion House, Bethal Square, Brecon,
Powys LD3 7AY
Tel: 01874 625708; Web: www.wildlifetrust.org.uk/brecknock

Gwent Wildlife Trust
Seddon House, Dingestow, Monmouth NP25 4DY
Tel: 01600 740600; Web: www.wildlifetrust.org.uk/gwent

Herefordshire Nature Trust
Lower House Farm, Ledbury Road, Tupsley, Hereford HR1 1UT
Tel: 01432 356872; Web: www.wildlifetrust.org.uk/hereford

Montgomeryshire Wildlife Trust
Collot House, 20 Severn Street, Welshpool, Powys SY21 7AD
Tel: 01938 555654; Web: www.montwt.co.uk/

North Wales Wildlife Trust
376 High Street, Bangor, Gwynedd LL57 1YE
Tel: 01248 351541; Web: www.wildlifetrust.org.uk/northwales

Radnorshire Wildlife Trust
Warwick House, High Street, Llandrindod Wells, Powys LD1 6AG
Tel: 01597 823298; Web: www.radnorshirewildlifetrust.org.uk

Shropshire Wildlife Trust
193 Abbey Foregate, Shrewsbury, Shropshire SY2 6AH
Tel: 01743 284280; Web: www.shropshirewildlifetrust.org.uk

Wye Valley Tourism
Web: www.wyevalleytourism.co.uk

Index

Illustrations and texts are indicated by italics